THE YOKE

AND THE ARROWS

THE YOKE

AND THE ARROWS

A REPORT ON SPAIN

HERBERT L. MATTHEWS

NEW YORK

GEORGE BRAZILLER, INC.

1957

© HERBERT L. MATTHEWS 1957

PRINTED IN THE UNITED STATES OF AMERICA

To Nancie—

now and always

Thanks are due, as always, to THE NEW YORK TIMES in whose service the material for this book was gathered over the past twenty-one years.

Not all the blood at Talavera shed,
Not all the marvels of Barossa's fight,
Not Albuera lavish of the dead,
Have won for Spain her well-asserted right.
When shall her Olive-Branch be free from blight?
When shall she breathe her from the blushing toil?
How many a doubtful day shall sink in night,
Ere the Frank robber turn him from his spoil,
And Freedom's stranger-tree grow native of the soil!

BYRON: *Childe Harold's Pilgrimage*

CONTENTS

THE YOKE

AND THE ARROWS

i.

THE BACKGROUND

ON JULY 18, 1936, THE WESTERN WORLD CROSSED A watershed that marked the end of one era and the beginning of another. A few generals in Spanish Morocco raised the standard of revolt, and the Spanish Civil War began.

Sometimes moments pregnant with fateful events are recognized, as the evening the lights went out all over Europe on August 4, 1914, or a quarter of a century later when Hitler attacked Poland. More often the historian, looking back, makes a mark on the calendar of the past and says: "A turning point came here."

The gesture is arbitrary. History, like nature, abhors a vacuum. There are no beginnings and no endings except creation and the Day of Judgment. The Spanish Civil War was an explosion at the end of a long powder train. We simplified it in our minds at the time, one way or another, but in reality it was an enormously complicated manifestation. It drew into itself all the threads of Spanish life and character, all the social conflicts that wrack our industrial age, all the

3

ideologies that soon were to be tearing the world apart, and that are still doing so.

Fortune, they say, is a jade. But so is history. It does the unaccountable. It takes men and turns them into fools—or heroes. There was a quality of madness about the Spanish Civil War that makes the children of the men and women in Spain who went through its fire look at their parents in wonder. How could they?

How could *we?* Which of us from, let us say, the age of thirty-eight or forty on, can forget the Spanish conflict if we had any political or religious consciousness in those three years from 1936 to 1939? It had quality, that war. Something in it reached deeply into our hearts as well as our minds. Old war horses like myself, old timers who went on following the lurid threads of the same pattern through the Second World War and into this time of troubles that we call the cold war, we still raise our heads, still feel a thrill deep inside thinking of those "far off things and battles long ago."

As World War II was ending I wrote: "I have already lived six years since the Spanish Civil War ended and have seen much of greatness and glory and many beautiful things and places since then, and I may, with luck, live another twenty or thirty years, but I know, as surely as I know anything in this world, that nothing so wonderful will ever happen to me again as those two and a half years I spent in Spain."

Yes, the Spanish Civil War had a special quality that the infinitely greater and more terrible World War II lacked. This was not just an episode in Spain's tormented history or an adventure in the lives of the men who went to Spain from many lands to fight for their ideologies or their ideals.

It was, among other things, a rehearsal for the World War, which those who were involved or interested could see coming.

4

At a meeting of the Cortes in Valencia on November 1, 1936, Francisco Largo Caballero, then the Premier, had said: "It is, indeed, a European war which is occurring here, and all of us are being plunged into it. We see the hour coming when a frightful world catastrophe will be unleashed. . . ."

I quoted those words in a book I wrote in the autumn of 1937 called *Two Wars and More to Come*—the other being Mussolini's Abyssian War that had ended as recently as May 5, 1936. It seemed so obvious to so many of us. This was part of the anguish suffered by those who interpreted the Spanish Civil War as a struggle of democracy against Fascism. We suffered because the Fascist side won, and had to win considering how the cards were stacked against the Spanish Republicans who were not only not helped by the major democracies—Britain, France and the United States—but were positively hamstrung by their prevailing appeasement of the Axis powers. This so-called policy of "non-intervention," fostered by the British and French, and the American arms embargo doomed the Madrid Government. That, too was predictable early in the Spanish War, but only those who felt its quality, only those who knew Spain and the Spanish character, were in a position to say that it would be a long, bitter, tenacious conflict fought to a finish.

Can we say that it is still being fought? What is victory? a modern Pontius Pilate might well ask. In World War II we crushed the German Nazis, the Italian Fascists, the Japanese Imperialists. We killed Hitler and Mussolini; we tamed the Emperor Hirohito. We crushed Germany, Italy and Japan. We did not kill totalitarianism, for the other Janus-head of that monster—communism—was our ally. We did not kill fascism, either, for ideas are not killed by bullets or even by hydrogen bombs. And in this year of 1957 Generalissimo

Francisco Franco is still to be reckoned with. The Spanish Civil War has not ended.

In a sense it could not end, any more than the Second World War ended. The same forces were at work, global forces, the fruition of a long history that, at the latest, began its modern phase with the American and French Revolutions. This is what made the Spanish Civil War so extraordinary, so ironical, so fateful. Spain was the last country where anyone looked for the first pangs of the travail that was to convulse Europe and the world. "Africa," they said, "began at the Pyrenees." Europe ended there, but the Spanish Civil War was a European war in miniature, even a world war.

The First World War was the last of an era that ended when those Spanish generals revolted on July 18, 1936. World War I has no more meaning to us today than the Napoleonic Wars. It was a war of conquest, a war of nations, a war of races, a war of survival, a war that not only had its roots in the past but that faced the past. Of all the sterile, useless wars in history it was the worst and the most frightful. Unhappily, it spawned some monsters. Out of its material destruction and spiritual horrors came men who gave expression to philosophies that had lain unnourished and despised in the womb of our times: Lenin and Stalin, Mussolini and Hitler, communism and fascism—all children of Marx, of 1848, of 1793, distortions and inversions of the noble principles that also brought liberalism and democracy.

The Fascist wing was militaristic, aggressive, nationalistic, racist. It attracted the militarism and nationalism of the dynamic Japanese. These two minor wars in Manchuria and Abyssinia were forerunners, harbingers of the evil to come. In themselves they could have been isolated. They were adventures, wars of conquest, naked aggressions, but because the

Abyssinian War was started and finished by a European Fascist dictator who lent his color to a simple act of national crime, it rates in history as a Fascist war, and so it is linked like a trigger to the conflict in which all the ideologies and all the new social and political forces were to get their first expression—the Spanish Civil War.

Why Spain should have been chosen to play this tragic role on the stage of modern history defies analysis. She was always capable of extremes, for a nation is the expression of its people and their character. In the late Middle Ages her philosophers and artists were the glory of Europe. Her merchants and bankers were among the wealthiest and the most able. However, they were mostly Moorish and Jewish; and the Catholic Spaniard (history gave the role to Ferdinand and Isabel) turned on them and drove them out of Spain.

The nation never recovered culturally or economically from that self-mutilation, but the interesting thing about the Spanish character is that the Spaniard did not care. On the contrary, he joined in the act and felt progressive as well as righteous. The year of the expulsion of the Jews was the same year as the discovery of America by Christopher Columbus.

There was no lack of greatness, for a few handfuls of conquistadores not only conquered a New World but founded a civilization that endures to this day. Latin America will never lose its Spanish imprint. Only England can boast a similar role in modern history.

The place of philosophy and the arts was taken by religion, in which Spanish faith and zeal, driven by Spanish extremism, not only converted a continent and a half to Christianity but gave the world St. Ignatius of Loyola. It also gave the world the sweeter and equally enduring figures of St. Theresa of Avila and St. John of the Cross, but these exist for us today, as they will forever, on a high mystic plane. The Jesuits are a living, practical force. They control education in Franco's Spain and much else besides. They are the authentic expression of Spanish extremism in its religious form. Although theirs is an Order with immense ramifications, there is no country in the world where they exercise such great national power as in Spain. Yet the Spaniards, on no less than six occasions since 1767 (the last in 1936), expelled their Jesuits and tried to suppress the Order. This was another kind of extremism at work.

What this points to, in a curious way, is the fact that Spain had isolated herself from Europe and from many of the trends that were shaping the modern world. Spain had no Reformation; all she had was a Counter Reformation which performed the negative role of preventing a Protestant movement. Philip II saw to that, and part of the price he paid was to isolate Spain from Europe.

The conquest and colonization of the New World brought fabulous riches in gold, silver and gems, but these added nothing to the real wealth of the nation. True national wealth, as we know today, lies in an educated, skillful, progressive people, in food, clothing, houses, farms, jobs and the comforts and amenities of life for the maximum number. It does not lie in dollar bills, stock certificates, bonds or Spanish gold doubloons for a handful of aristocrats and adventurers. The wealth of the New World masked the essential poverty of the Spanish people, a poverty that exists to this day. And the source of that wealth—the whole New World—crumbled away from Spain under the winds of liberty blown by the ideas of the American and French Revolutions.

Yet out of the darkness and misery, it was Spain and the Spanish people that gave expression to the new forces of liberty which were to strive against the forces of reaction in the first half of the nineteenth century. This was the recurrent paradox of Spanish history at work again. The first defeat of a Napoleonic Army in Europe took place at Bailén in Andalucia in Spain on July 23, 1808. It was the Spanish people —not the generals, aristocrats or monarchy—allied to the English in the Peninsular War, who so bled the Napoleonic forces that they were weakened for the campaign in the East. It was the meeting of the Cortes in Cadiz in 1812 that drew up the first truly liberal constitution on the European continent. The word "liberal" and the political philosophy of liberalism came out of the Spain of that time.

The genius is there. So is the spirit. So is the urge to freedom. But they are not universal. The rulers of Spain since Ferdinand and Isabel have been the traditionalists—the kings, the aristocrats, the generals and the priests. Each time the people rose or freedom asserted itself, one or the other of them, or all together, would clamp the lid back again. This is what happened after the Napoleonic War when a perfidious and wicked king—Ferdinand VII—returned to his throne. That is what happened in 1939 when a *caudillo*—Generalissimo Francisco Franco—slammed another lid down and sat on it.

Perhaps this is begging the question, for the kings and *caudillos*, the grandees and cardinals are just as truly Spanish as the professor who demands freedom or the peasant who demands land. It is so often argued that Spaniards are unfit or unready for democracy. If so, who is to blame but the ruling classes who failed to educate and prepare their people for freedom? But if so, how explain the fact that the first people in Europe to fight fascism were the Spanish? It could be argued that no European people are so radical, for a great many Spaniards are against authority, against the Army, against the rich, against landowners and employers and even, to a considerable extent, against the clergy. The ferocity of the Civil War was more than an expression of the Spanish character when aroused. It was a revolutionary ferment. One of the aims of the rebellion by the generals was to crush the upsurge of workers and peasants.

Spaniards, themselves, were far more concerned with their internal social and economic conflict than with the struggle of ideologies that was imposed upon them. They played their global role half-heartedly. Every familiar label from abroad was turned in practice into something peculiarly Spanish. There were Socialists, Anarchists, Communists, Fascists (i.e. Falangists), Republicans, Monarchists, Catholics (in the political sense), and, of course, all the small letter words— liberals, democrats, conservatives, nationalists, progressives, reactionaries. Every one of them was so colored by the Spanish character and Spanish history and traditions that the labels were more confusing than helpful.

The Spanish Civil War was, indeed, "an international war fought on national soil," but it was much more than that. We, looking back today and revisiting the Spain we knew in the lurid, passionate days of the 1930's, can see now that even those who fought in the name of anti-fascism or anti-communism were at least in part rationalizing their emotions. What lingers today is the profoundly Spanish character of the conflict. That was hard for us foreigners to understand at the time; we were all caught up in the ideological struggle of our era. Besides, it was easy for us to understand terms like fascism, communism, liberalism, democracy, appeasement, imperialism, racism and the like. These forces were occupying the forefront of the world stage. They swept like tides over every shore, but now the tide has receded and the eternal outlines of the land it covered are revealed once again in Spain.

This is no attempt to deny the reality of those forces. Spain, after all, was their major battle ground for nearly three years; but Spain remains in this year 1957, and so do the Spanish people, and if one says that in a sense the Spanish Civil War has not yet ended it is because Spaniards placed themselves at the head of these movements in 1936, won or lost in their names, and still today interpret what happened in terms of those battle slogans.

Because the Rebels or Nationalists won and the Republicans or Loyalists lost, and because we are so frightened of communism today, a myth has been created: the Loyalists were "Reds" and Spain was saved from communism by Generalissimo Francisco Franco and his German and Italian allies. No one can prove what might have happened if Franco had been defeated, but the facts are that there was precious little communism in Spain when the Civil War started and the Republican Government was at no time "Red."

This is not a history of modern Spain or of the Spanish Civil War, but certain facts must be kept in mind if we are to understand the situation today. Many, many Spaniards since the Civil War and now justify what General Franco and the other rebel generals did, but those who know what the situation was like in 1936 do not do so in terms of anti-communism.

There were only sixteen Communist deputies in a Cortes of 473 when the Civil War began, and no Communists in the Government. The deputies were elected on February 16, 1936, at which time Communist party headquarters made the exaggerated claim that it had 35,000 members. Those deputies became part of a Popular Front of Socialists and Republicans that my newspaper, *The New York Times,* estimated at 269 in all. Republican Spain had no diplomatic relations with the Soviet Union, so there was no Russian Ambassador or Embassy in Madrid when the war began in July. Marcel Rosenberg, the first Ambassador, arrived on August 27, six weeks after the fighting started.

General Franco had German and Italian arms and technicians from the beginning of the war. Russian technicians and arms did not come along until October. The *Survey of International Affairs,* which Arnold J. Toynbee edited in 1936, as he still does, for the Royal Institute of International Affairs, estimated that when the war began in July the orthodox Communists in Spain numbered 50,000. (Spain had its Trotskyites and its dissident Communists of various shades in an organization known as the POUM, but these, of course, had no relations with Moscow.)

The Communists grew in strength and influence as the war progressed, but at this point we are merely discussing the myth that the revolt against the Republican Government in July 1936 was a patriotic uprising to save Spain from communism. General Franco issued a manifesto as he was leaving his post in the Canary Islands for Morocco to start the rebellion. He did not mention communism.

To be fair and to keep the record straight, it must be made equally clear that the Loyalists were not, at the time, saving Spain from the sort of fascism represented by Germany and Italy. The argument here is less obvious and more subtle, because, after all, Spain has a type of fascist government today, and has had one since the Franco forces won the Civil War. Yet, as will be seen, Spaniards here, as always, were taking something with a foreign label and making a peculiarly

Spanish product out of it. What we all believed in 1936—I mean those who sympathized with the Republicans—was clearly wrong.

We were fooled by the fact that José Antonio Primo de Rivera, son of the dictator of Spain from 1923 to 1930, founded the Falange in 1933 on Italian Fascist lines, with a dash of clericalism. He used the same technique of agitation and terrorism by gangs of bullies (in Italy they were the *Squadristi*), talked of a corporate state, of the glories of combat, of hierarchy and discipline. It was fascism all right, and the violence he unleashed did much to bring on the chaos and ultimate explosion of July 18. The Falangists helped to make anything but civil war impossible. The issue had to be fought out, but it is obvious to us now that neither José Antonio nor the Falange was ever going to get control of Spain even if his side won. This was a military *pronunciamiento* in the good old Spanish style, and the leader was to be a *caudillo*, or military chieftain, such as Spain had known often since the Napoleonic Wars. The dominance of the Army began a century and a half ago and is yet to end. Under true fascism the Army is the instrument of the Fascist state. In Spain the Falange (the Fascist party) was never more than an instrument of the Caudillo Franco. The failure to make this distinction has caused unending confusion.

In the years from 1933 to 1936, the Falange served the Army by helping to create the anarchy which gave the generals their excuse for stepping in, but Franco made it clear enough for those who could see that he was going to be the boss—not the Falange. In fact, the movement became an astonishing hodge-podge in the Civil War and has never been anything else. Its full title is *Falange Española Tradicionalista y de las J.O.N.S.* (J.O.N.S. stands for *Juntas Obreras*—some-

times written *Juntas Ofensivas—Nacional Sindicalistas.*) The
J.O.N.S. was founded a year before the Falange, and was more
the type of German national socialism. In 1937, during the
Civil War, Franco arranged a shotgun wedding with the
Traditionalists, or Carlists, from the intensely Catholic prov-
ince of Navarre. The two forces were bitter enemies.

Since the generals had no ideology or political philosophy,
Falangism had to provide one and in this way, also, it served
a useful purpose for General Franco; it also served to confuse
all of us. But let it be well understood today that the Republicans were no more saving Spain from what we understood
as fascism in 1936, than the Rebels were saving Spain from
communism.

The Civil War, I repeat, was profoundly Spanish. This was
its basic characteristic to Spaniards—and it still is. For us, it
is the form given to the conflict by the clash of totalitarianism
and democracy that is important; it is the fact that Spain became a battlefield for the ideologies of our time, that it was
a rehearsal for World War II, that for three years it was the
hub of the universe—these are the features that strike us today, as they did at the time. But Spaniards do not think of
their Civil War in such terms. To them, it was Spanish history
that reached a tragic climax in 1936, not world history. And,
of course, both points of view are justified. The contemporary
world being what it is, and conflicts being impossible to isolate, even a civil war becomes a world war. That is what happened in China, in Korea and in Indo-China in the past decade.
Each in its way was a world conflict at the same time that it
was a civil war. Spain was the prototype, which was one
reason for its historic importance.

In the days of its autocratic monarchs (Philip II, 1527-

1598, was the last with any pretensions to greatness), Spain seemed to have a form of government that suited her people. It was despotic, aristocratic, clerical and military. With the New World it represented an empire such as only Rome, and later England, could match in world history.

With the decline of power and wealth, and the isolationism from the liberal, popular, industrial trends of the modern world, Spain's governmental and social structures became anachronisms. And because so much of this traditionalism kept its strength, because it rose successfully in 1936, because it is still represented by the regime of Generalissimo Francisco Franco, Spain has remained something of an anomaly in the contemporary world. Only now is this isolationism breaking down, and it is thrilling to see.

The Civil War of 1936-1939 was a struggle of the forces of modernism against traditionalism. This, at least, was one of its meanings, and one of its most important meanings. It explains why the victory of Franco and the Nationalists, however decisive in the last eighteen years, is essentially a hollow one. Franco slammed a lid down and sat on it; but the social, political, intellectual and economic forces of the twentieth century continued to swell and ferment, and they are the ones that will ultimately triumph. A few decades are a long time in the lives of a generation but they are a second or two in the life of a nation.

The cruel blow struck against the pitiful remnants of Spanish power in 1898, with the loss of Cuba and the Philippines, brought a reaction at home that was represented by a handful of intellectuals known since as the "Generation of '98." They brought the ideas of modern liberalism to Spain which culminated in the Revolution of 1931 that overthrew the monarchy of Alfonso XIII and established the Second Republic. (There had been a premature and disastrous First Republic in 1873.)

Despite his constant harping on communism, Franco knew that his real enemy was liberalism—and he still knows it. He has again and again avowed his intention of ridding Spain of "liberalism," which to his military mind is synonymous with a nineteenth century *laissez-faire* libertarianism. His motto is: "Discipline and Unity."

The political drive for freedom also had its social and economic aspects. It was not going to be possible for a few generals, aristocrats, landowners and businessmen, supported by the Church, to keep a people in poverty and ignorance, without their land to till, without the right to organize labor unions, to strike for higher wages and better conditions, to educate their children in the professions, and, in the long run, to conduct their own government.

A strong central government run by an elite and headed by a Caudillo could, in theory, give the people all they wanted —land, jobs, houses, a higher standard of living, a good education, peace, discipline and unity. However, human nature, original sin, a lack of suitable officials, the urge to liberty, the ferment of modern ideas and innumerable other dispositions and forces make such an "ideal" government impossible.

Above all in Spain! The Spaniard is individualistic, proud, courageous and unruly. He conforms to no pattern; he fits no mold; he shuns moderation. Like the Poles and Hungarians who rose against the Russians, the Spaniards have no hesitation in sacrificing their lives to a just cause.

Hundreds of thousands of them did exactly that in the Civil War of 1936-1939. You may say that they were wrong, stupid, foolish, mad, misguided. Or you may think them heroic and instinctively wise. Perhaps quixotic? Who, better than Spaniards have a right to tilt at windmills.

The forces came to a head; the volcano erupted; the Civil War began.

ii.

THE CIVIL WAR

A CIVIL WAR IS THE MOST TERRIBLE OF ALL WARS. WE Americans know that. There is something especially fierce, bitter and tragic about a civil war, something desperate and maddening. The Spaniards have a cruel streak in them, and a disdain for death. They have unlimited courage, but it is of a passionate type—not the disciplined bravery of the Germans and Anglo-Saxons.

The Spanish Civil War was not geographic like our War Between the States. It cut across all lines; it literally pitted brother against brother; it spared no families; it blanketed every city, town and village in its first fierce outburst. Then, in time, it did become geographic as the Rebel forces conquered the western and then northern parts of the Peninsula. And finally the Republicans were driven into France or overwhelmed where they stood.

All Spain suffered, and so did every Spaniard—some member of the family killed or wounded, property destroyed or damaged, relatives imprisoned and sometimes tortured, shortages of food and other necessities, a general state of terror. So it went for nearly three years. A generation was branded, a nation horribly mutilated, and the aftermath had its own special quality of bitterness and pain.

No doubt the oft-mentioned figure of 1,000,000 Spaniards killed was somewhat exaggerated. No one will ever know. Casualty figures were not kept, and it is only too likely that more men and women were killed in acts of terror and executions than in acts of war.

The atrocities were a well-advertised horror on both sides. There was nothing to choose between them. The Loyalist side got the worst of it in the battle of propaganda because in the first wild, mad popular reaction, the flaming passions of anticlericalism were uncontrollable. So many priests and nuns were slain and so many churches burned and sacked in the first days of the war that the world was properly horrified. These atrocities, and the belief that the Loyalists were turning Spain into a Communist state, led Pope Pius XI to side openly with General Franco almost from the beginning. So did a great majority of Roman Catholics in the United States, who remain pro-Franco to this day.

The Church problem in Spain is complicated and delicate, and those of us who have tried for twenty years to discuss it with frankness and honesty have to bear a great deal of abuse and face a great deal of misunderstanding. Yet it is a subject that must be treated, and will be.

At the moment, what is under discussion is this matter of atrocities, because the grievous wounds of that terrorism on the Spanish people are not yet entirely healed. For those who hold all human life sacred, for those to whom a worker in a factory or a peasant in a field has as much right to live as a priest, the Rebel atrocities had their own peculiar horror.

Where the mobs on the Loyalist side killed in blind, ignorant passion, the killings by the Insurgents often had a cold, calculated quality. I think we ought to say: "A plague o' both your houses" in this matter of atrocities. They concern us because of the enduring mark they made, and because they help us to understand what a Spanish phenomenon the Civil War was.

Of course, a certain amount of the killing on the Republican side was political—Communists against Anarchists, Stalinists against Trotskyites and the like; but this type of gang warfare was not important, and it often involved foreigners in the International Brigade. What counted was Spaniard killing Spaniard. On the Loyalist side it stopped early in the war; on the Rebel side it went on for the obvious reason that the Nationalists conquered town after town and village after village as the war progressed, and in each place a toll was taken.

Hatred is a terrible quality when it is nourished for many years. Civil wars take a long time to forget. It was easier for the Americans to forgive the Japanese, or the British the Germans, after 1945 than it was for the Spaniards to forgive each other after 1939.

Passions had been aroused well before the war began. Spain was a nation badly torn by internal strife for at least five years before July 1936. From any point of view, the Second Republic, which began with the flight of King Alfonso XIII in April, 1931, was a colossal failure. One might be sympathetic and say that it had high ideals but was never given a chance to achieve them, thanks to the generals, the reactionary fascists and the foreign intriguers; or one might be unsympathetic and say that it was a weak, quarrelsome, incompetent Government, falling into the hands of Communists who took advice from Moscow.

There is truth and falsehood in both pictures. The one feature that really made all the difference was the weakness of the Republican Government. Had it been able to maintain law and order, there would, of course, have been no Civil War and no possible justification for what happened. The charge that the Republicans were planning or would have succumbed to a Communist revolution is nonsense. As was stated before, the Spanish Communists were of no importance before the war or when it began. The Republican leaders were good men in the moral sense, well-intentioned, liberal and democratic. The trouble was that they could not rule. This is begging the question since the real problem is why they could not keep the peace and run Spain as a democracy. The answer is long and complicated, and many books have already been written on the subject. I would particularly recommend *The Spanish Labyrinth*, by Gerald Brenan, published in 1943.

For our purpose it is enough to keep in mind that a great deal of Spanish history was coming to an explosive climax. Foreign intrigue, at this point, was of no importance. The decisive roles were played by social and economic forces, complicated by clericalism and regionalism. Spanish isolationism had helped to build up volcanic forces. A nation of passionate people that had no Protestant Reformation and no Enlightenment, and that lagged generations behind the rest of Europe in the social and industrial fields, could hardly avoid exploding. There had been two grave civil wars in the nineteenth century: 1833-1839 and 1870-1876. There had been outbursts of anti-clericalism as murderous as those of 1936 in 1835 and 1909.

The Spanish peasant never, generally speaking, owned the land he tilled or enough of it to provide a decent living. He was—and still is—kept in grinding poverty on land often

owned by absentee aristocrats. The average Spanish employer
—and this is still true to a considerable extent—was a capi-
talist in the Marxist sense: he exploited his workers for his
own personal gain.

The landowners and the employers were supported by
the Army and the Church. All four supported the Monarchy
as long as it lasted and tried to make the Monarchy a shield
to protect their interests. But the protection was against the
people—the peasants, the workers and the intellectuals. And
it was the intellectual—the middle-class professional man—
who made the Republican Revolution of 1931, and it was he
who tried and failed to make a go of the Second Republic.

With the Monarchy gone, what were the landowners,
the businessmen, the bishops and the generals to do? For the
most part, the first three groups did the honorable thing and
formed a conservative, clerical and—it must be stated—somewhat reactionary opposition to the liberal Government. The
generals bided their time and then plotted rebellion.

Meanwhile, the country ran a deadly course from violence
to chaos. Spain does not have a national mold. In a sense, the
British Isles had the same problem; but, except for Catholic
Irishmen, Britain was able to create a united people out of
the English, the Welsh, the Scots and the Ulstermen. Italy was
divided until 1870, and the Piedmontese are as different from
the Sicilians as the Basques are from the Andalucians. Yet
the trend in Italy was toward centralization in Rome; the
trend in Spain was centrifugal—away from Madrid.

The regional forces tore at Spain's heart. They resented
the domination of Madrid, and still do. Catalonia and the
Basque country have their own languages and culture, and
they are racially different from the "true" Spaniard of Aragon
and Castile. Because the Second Republic was willing to grant

them their *fueros,* or autonomous rights, the Catalans and Basques sided with the Loyalists in the Civil War. Since the Basque country was intensely religious, this was an embarrassment to those who saw the war as the God-fearing against the Godless. General Franco's forces, incidentally, executed about twenty Basque priests after they conquered the region.

All this is simply by way of explaining that it really was a *Spanish* Civil War. And it was started by the Spanish generals. In his book, *The Spanish Tragedy,* the late Professor E. Allison Peers of Liverpool University, who was a serious historian and an expert on Spain, and who was very friendly to the Franco side, calls the beginning of the Civil War "a military revolt . . . a revolution carefully planned and skilfully organized by able military leaders on a nation-wide scale."

However, the issue was decided by foreign intervention: on Franco's side by the Germans and Italians and by the equally important negative effects of "non-intervention" by Britain and France, backed by the American arms embargo. Of this there can be no question, for the quantitive and qualitative aid from Nazi Germany and Fascist Italy far outweighed the help that the Loyalists got from Russia. This can easily be documented.

Russian help started late and ended long before the war drew to its close. What matériel Spain got from Moscow was paid for, at generous prices, in gold. There were never any Russian troops in Spain, whereas at the time of the Battle of Guadalajara alone, in March, 1937, Italy had four full divisions in Spain. Russia sent advisers and technicians—the latter to run the tanks and planes until Spaniards could be trained to handle them. The advisers—military and political—stayed almost to the end, but judging from the results one can hardly claim that they were very effective.

The French sold some planes and arms early in the war, and permitted a good deal of the Russian arms to go through French territory; but since it was France, along with Britain, which put over the "non-intervention" policy, it certainly cannot be claimed that France helped the Loyalists. On the contrary, if there was any one feature that lost the war for the Loyalists, it was this Anglo-French "non-intervention." Mussolini, on the other hand, was to write in the *Popolo d'Italia* of May 20, 1938: "We have intervened from the first to the last moment."

The role played by the United States added a fatal touch. It was the era of isolationism here, as it was the era of appeasement in Europe. The policy, insofar as any one man was responsible for it, was made by Secretary of State Cordell Hull. President Franklin D. Roosevelt was in his heart and mind in favor of the Loyalists, but he played politics and allowed his convictions to be overruled. The full story, for those interested, is to be found in a recent doctoral thesis by F. Jay Taylor, called "The United States and the Spanish Civil War." Dr. Taylor cites what Mrs. Eleanor Roosevelt wrote in her book *This I Remember:* "Franklin frequently refrained from supporting causes in which he believed because of political realities," she said. "There were times when this annoyed me very much. In the case of the Spanish Civil War, for instance, we had to remain neutral, though Franklin knew quite well he wanted the democratic government to be successful."

In my own book *The Education of a Correspondent*, I took a sardonic pleasure in quoting what former Undersecretary of State Sumner Welles wrote in *The Time for Decision*, that "of all our blind isolationist policies, the most disastrous was our attitude on the Spanish Civil War."

The most statesmanlike document on the subject of our arms embargo at the time came in a long letter from former Secretary of State Henry L. Stimson to the Editor of *The New York Times*, which we published on January 24, 1939. Mr. Stimson made a number of telling points:

"The Republican Government of Spain has been recognized as the true Government of Spain by our Government. . . . One of the most important of these rights which a state like Spain is entitled to expect from another Government, which has recognized it as a friendly neighbor in the family of nations, is the right of self-defense against any future rebellions which may challenge its authority.

"Such a nation [has] the exclusive right . . . to purchase the necessary supplies and munitions for the purpose of putting down the rebellion."

We insisted on such a right, Mr. Stimson pointed out, in our own Civil War. Writing of "non-intervention" he said:

"The first thing to be said about this agreement was that it was a complete abandonment of a code of practise which the international world had adopted through preceding ages. . . . The non-intervention agreement at once became a mockery and a failure. . . .

"The results have shown how futile as well as dangerous novel experiments in international law can be. The United States on its part has abandoned a traditional policy to which for a century and a half it had carefully adhered as a means of protecting the peace and stability of nations, which like itself, preferred to live not armed to the teeth. It is likely sorely to rue the day when that principle was abandoned and when it consented to a new precedent which may hereafter weight the scale in favor of a militaristic and thoroughly armed nation. . . .

"If this Loyalist Government is overthrown, it is evident now that its defeat will be solely due to the fact that it has been deprived of its right to buy from us and from other friendly nations the munitions necessary for its defense."

This was the voice of a true and wise American and it will be the judgment of history.

American popular sentiment was in favor of the Loyalists and became increasingly so as the war progressed. Toward the end, Gallup polls showed that 76 per cent of the Americans who expressed an opinion on the Civil War favored the Loyalists. This must have included many Roman Catholics. Dr. Taylor cites a survey of the American Institute of Public Opinion taken among Catholics which showed 30 per cent for the Republicans, 31 per cent neutral and only 39 per cent pro-Franco.

However, there is no denying the fact that the Spanish Civil War divided Americans along religious lines. In this respect it was one of the most remarkable and disturbing phenomena in our history. No other foreign event had ever had that effect, which is one more evidence of the intensity of the emotions that Spain aroused.

Those emotions are by no means dead. Whenever my newspaper prints a critical editorial on the Franco regime, whenever dispatches and articles appear that describe unfavorable events in Spain there are indignant and sometimes abusive letters to the Editor or to the offending correspondent. When a section of the American people feels strongly on any particular subject, as the Irish did on independence and partition or the Jews on Palestine, the political pressure on Washington is always effective. The combination of a powerful Catholic lobby in Washington and the prevailing isolationism were more than enough to keep the United States "neutral" in the Spanish Civil War and to maintain the arms embargo.

It was not enough to keep some 5,000 young Americans from volunteering to fight in Spain—and not only Americans and not only the young. The International Brigade formed a unique phenomenon in modern history. To those of us who were there, who knew the men, who saw them fight and die, they brought a glory and enrichment to the life of our times. The record was later blurred and smeared by the hysterical form that anti-communism took after the Second World War, particularly during the horrors of McCarthyism in the United States; but history will set the record straight.

Perhaps not in our time. The lives, the passions, the hopes —sometimes one wonders if they had all been in vain. Sometimes I think either we were mad and foolish and quite wrong, or the world has simply forgotten in the rush of greater and more recent preoccupations.

I once wrote of the Brigaders as "the finest group of men I ever knew or hope to know in my life." They were that, even though in the years after the war only the Stalinist Communists perpetuated their memory and dominated their organizations. The Brigaders who made their mark in the post-war years were almost all Communists.

Some were liquidated like Laszlo Raik, Hungarian Foreign Minister, and Traicho Kostov, Bulgarian Prime Minister. They were too independent and were caught in the Titoist purges of 1949. Then there was "General Walter" of the 35th Division, a first rate commander who one knew was Polish, but that was all. He turned out to be Colonel General Karol Swierczewski of the Polish Army, Vice-Minister of Defense in Warsaw's Communist Government. Ukrainian terrorists assassinated him in March 1947.

Most of the Russians sent to Spain ended up in prison,

in Siberia, or were executed during the great purges of 1937-1938. They could not be trusted after their experiences.

The Italian leaders managed to stick it out and are all "big shots" now: Palmiro Togliatti, the head of the Italian Communist party; Pietro Nenni, the fellow-travelling Socialist; Luigi Longo (Gallo), who led the partisans in Northern Italy during our World War II campaign; Guiseppe di Vittorio (Nicoletti), now head of the Italian General Confederation of Labor; Vittorio Vidali (Carlos Contreras), the Communist leader in Trieste.

The best of them all was anti-communist—Randolfo Pacciardi, who commanded the Garibaldini Battalion at Madrid and on the Jarama River in the early months of the war and then broke with the I.B. leaders because of their militant and too exclusive communism. What he learned in those days stood him in good stead later as Premier De Gasperi's Minister of War. One reason communism has been held in check in Italy is to be found in the person and the experience of Pacciardi.

One of the bad ones, for my money, was André Marty, the French Communist leader who died last year. He was the Number One man of the I.B., and Ernest Hemingway only exaggerated a little in the bitter caricature that is to be found in *For Whom the Bell Tolls*. My favorite Frenchman was André Malraux, a true idealist and a brave man—they were pretty well all brave, for that matter. Malraux headed a group of French aviators who nearly all got themselves killed at the beginning of the war flying the crates that the Government picked up second hand, anywhere it could. Malraux has been consistent—a Brigader, a partisan in World War II, and now a De Gaullist, and through it all a great artist. I cannot believe he regrets the Spanish episode in a notable life.

Neither did George Orwell. Those who read *Homage to Catalonia* too hastily, or did not know how to judge it properly, or that Orwell had altered his opinions somewhat later on, think of Orwell as one who "exposed" the Loyalist Government and unmasked the Communists.

Orwell's experience in Spain only lasted from December 1936, to May 1937. It covered a narrow and abnormal sector of the Aragon front, ending in Barcelona during an uprising that he never understood. He fought as a volunteer with a militia outfit formed by the weird, thoroughly eccentric and untrustworthy organization known as the P.O.U.M. Orwell was as brilliant, as honest and courageous as any man could be; but his politics were completely impractical, and his knowledge of what was really happening was slight. He got caught up in the partisan politics of Loyalist Spain and got caught on the wrong side—in fact, on a bad side. He was the victim of the ignorance of his idealism. It was a harsh and soul-trying experience for him. He was severely wounded, pursued by the police and barely succeeded in fleeing to France. Yet, he could still write from outside:

"It sounds like lunacy, but the thing that both of us wanted [his wife was with him] was to be back in Spain. . . . Curiously enough the whole experience has left me with not less but more belief in the decency of human beings."

Orwell confessed to "partisanship, mistakes of fact and the distortion inevitably caused by my having seen only one corner of events," but still it was "a state of affairs worth fighting for." Spain worked its magic on Orwell as it did on all of us.

Incidentally, although he was with a Spanish militia outfit, not the International Brigades, his motives in going to Spain and fighting for the Loyalists were the same as those of all the true volunteers. How many of the Communists were really volunteers, and how many were ordered to Spain by their party leaders, could never be known. My estimate was that 80 per cent of the Brigaders were Communists and that, nevertheless, most of these were genuine volunteers. It was one of the most significant aspects of the Civil War that there were no genuine volunteers whatever on the Franco side except a very small, rather comical Irish group in the early months of the conflict.

It is a fair question, knowing how preponderantly Communist the International Brigade was, why one could retain such a high regard for the Brigaders and their organization. Most people in the post-war period think of the Communists as if their position and the place of communism in the world were the same in 1936-1939 as in 1946-1957. In so doing, we are conveniently inclined to forget that Soviet Russia and the Communists were our allies in World War II and that the war in Europe could not have been won without them.

This did not mean that those who understood communism, or how the Russians really felt, had any illusions. Some of us started writing as early as 1944 about the fairly obvious fact that the post-war era would find the Soviet Union and the United States lined up as the world champions of totalitarianism and democracy. A liberal in Spain, such as I considered myself to be, had many a long and inconclusive argument with the Communists, who were, of course, proselytizers. However, it stood to reason that a liberal could not be a Communist or turn into one. These two political philosophies are contradictions, and it is logically impossible to reconcile them.

Nevertheless, in the Spanish Civil War, as in the World War, the liberal and the Communist were on the same side. They were fighting in a just cause to win a war that liberals and democrats should have wanted to see won. The fact that the Reds would have tried to seize power after the war, and were, indeed, trying to do so during the war, had exactly the same relevance on a small scale as the Communists' obvious intention after World War II to achieve a world revolution. It meant that one had to be on one's guard and prepared, but meanwhile the problem was to win the war. This, incidentally, was what George Orwell completely missed. He wanted to win the social revolution and the war at the same time.

It is the fate of all revolutions to move to the right, which Orwell knew as well as anybody, although he seems illogically to have resented the fact in Spain. He knew all the answers; they are to be found in his book; but he was personally too much of a rebel at heart to accept the inevitable without protest. What he saw as an evil and a pity was in reality a necessity. "As far as my purely personal preferences went, I would have liked to join the Anarchists," he wrote. He was the individual, the libertarian at heart, but the war could not possibly be won by such men or such doctrines. In a sense, Orwell was one of the children that the revolution devoured; he could not be expected to like the process.

The Communists in Spain, whatever one thought of communism, were loyal to the Republican Government. It was the time of Popular Fronts in Europe, and the Reds knew perfectly well they could not unify Loyalist Spain under their banner. They were the most disciplined and the best trained of the Loyalist troops, and they were the only ones who fought to the end in the Madrid sector. Their leaders, such as Lister, Modesto, Galán and El Campesino, were the best to come up in the war. They were willing—for tactical reasons, of course —to play down the social, proletarian revolution until the war was over. This made them, in a sense, counter-revolutionaries, which astonished and horrified George Orwell and many like him. If he had known more about communism at the time, he would have realized that it is basically and always counterrevolutionary to a considerable degree. After all, it is a totalitarian movement. The dictatorship of the proletariat is pie in the sky; meanwhile, there is state socialism and a hierarchical structure that is as little egalitarian as an absolute monarchy.

Don Juan Negrín, the Republican Premier in the last half of the Civil War, was no more Communist than you or I. He was nominally a Socialist, but the Spanish Socialists were not Marxists any more than the British Laborites. Dr. Negrín's problem was to win the war, or at least to hold on until the outbreak of the European war, which he and all of us saw coming. He could not continue the war or hold Republican Spain together without the Spanish Communists or without help from Russia, the only country willing to sell him arms and one of the few standing up for Loyalist Spain in the League of Nations.

To argue from this that Dr. Negrín was a Red or even a fellow-traveller is nonsense. The Negrín Government was never dominated by the Reds. To argue, as so many people did and do, that Spain would have gone Communist later if the Republicans had won, is, in my opinion, just as far from the mark. No one can prove what might have happened in such a hypothetical case. One can only pass an opinion. Personally, I am convinced that Spain would not have gone Communist, and I think the best evidence of this is what happened in Europe after the Second World War.

The Russians could not establish communism in any country where they were unable to exert the force of their arms. The Soviet bloc is a solid one. Even in Italy and France, with their large Communist movements, it proved impossible to establish Communist regimes. Spain was much further removed geographically.

This is aside from the fact that the internal difficulties would have been enormous. The Spaniard is even "worse" material for communism than the Italian was for fascism. A Communist regime could only be set up in Spain if the Russians overran the whole of Western Europe, which they did not do and which we may trust they will never do.

But let us get back to the International Brigaders. I said they were "the finest group of men I ever knew or ever hoped to know in my life." I was not, of course, thinking of every Brigader, of men like André Marty or Vittorio Vidali. I was thinking first of the 20 per cent who were liberals, anti-Fascists, idealists. Many of these sacrificed their lives or were maimed in the fight against fascism for freedom and democracy.

This was equally true of a great many of the Communists, and I am now thinking particularly of the American Communists whom I knew best. You can say today that they were mistaken or naïve. A lot of them realized that fact when Stalin got together with Hitler in 1939 and stayed together until the Fuehrer turned and attacked Russia. Some have taken all this time, until the Russians brutally crushed the Hungarian uprising in October 1956, to realize what Russian communism really means. I feel, and have always felt, that such men were tragically mistaken; I never felt that they were evil. The idealistic appeal of communism to hundreds of millions of good and sincere men in the world has been one of its great strengths. If such men saw or understood the evils of communism they would naturally abhor it.

We are talking here of the years 1936-1939, when these issues were not nearly so clear as they are today and when communism—again for tactical reasons—was anti-fascist. So far as foreign intervention on the Loyalist side in Spain was concerned, the keynote was anti-fascism. Are we forgetting what a real and deeply felt emotion the hatred of fascism was in the 1930's? In the few years preceding the Spanish Civil War, fascism had won great victories in Germany, Austria and Abyssinia and was dangerously entrenched in Italy. A few months after the Civil War ended the European democracies were involved in a life and death struggle against the fascist powers, one that we were later to join.

The history of a period, the true facts and the atmosphere in which they happened, must not and cannot honestly be rewritten simply because we now hold other ideas about the forces involved or because we possess the convenient instrument of hindsight. Such rewriting can be left to the Communists and fascists who make their histories conform to the political conveniences of the moment. It would be dishonest to write and think of the Spanish Civil War in any other terms than what really did happen and the way that we felt then. The mistakes need correction—and Lord knows we all made plenty of them—but the truth does not change.

The Spanish Civil War did not turn out as most of us hoped. Loyalist Spain did not exemplify all the desires and ideals we harbored in those years. One way or another, there was cause for bitterness and disappointment. The good and the bad were so mixed—mixed with all the sins that flesh is heir to, especially plain, unvarnished inefficiency, pettiness and mistakes. It was all a mess, one grand and glorious mess; but really glorious in some ways amid all the tragedy.

Men like George Orwell cried out because they thought that the impossible could happen in Spain, that Utopia could have been built then and there. Spain had a quality in the

Civil War which made people feel that way. The heartbreak had to come; a tragedy was being enacted, not a comedy and still less an idyll. Orwell saw only a little of the war in time and place, but he caught all its greatness. That is why he wrote: "I wish I could convey to you the atmosphere of that time."

I, too, had that wish in the Spanish Civil War, doubtless with more passion than an American war correspondent should have felt. However, I held back no facts and wrote only what I saw or believed to be true. In my creed of journalism, this is all that can fairly be asked. To ask that a correspondent have no feelings or ideas or even prejudices and bias of his own is asking the impossible. We, too, are human.

Perhaps I was tragically wrong. I do not think so. No one will ever persuade me, for instance, that the men who came from all over the world to fight in Spain were clever or cynical or hypocritical, or that they were mere robots obeying orders (except for the few Russian leaders involved). I still say they fought against fascism and—at the time— for the democracy we know. I still say that a vast majority of them fought and died for the highest sort of moral principles.

Like Orwell, although for different reasons, I came out of the war heartsick; but, like him, I had learned some lessons. They seemed worth a great deal. All of us—liberals, democrats, anti-fascists—had, in a sense, fought and lost.

On the day Barcelona fell to the Navarrese, the Moors, the Germans and Italians, Mussolini went out on the balcony of the Palazzo Venezia and cried to the throng that had been duly herded in the square: "Your shout of exultation, which is fully justified, blends with that rising in all the cities of Spain which are now completely liberated from the Reds' infamies and with the shout of joy from all anti-Bolshevists the world over. General Franco's magnificent troops and our fearless Legionaries have not only beaten Negrín's Government, but many others of our enemies are now biting the dust."

That was fair enough, so to speak. We did, indeed, bite the dust, we Americans and British and French. If Mussolini was gloating a little too soon, it was not thanks to us but to the Spanish Republicans who fought so long and so hard against impossible odds that Italy was too weak to join Germany when World War II started. Ciano was constrained to tell Ribbentrop that for three years Italy would not be again in a position to fight. She only entered the war when Duce mistakenly felt sure that it was all but over, and she never could put up a fight.

In assessing the place of the Spanish Civil War in contemporary history, that is something to keep in mind. Some of the things we correspondents wrote in those years may not seem too ridiculous to the historians of later generations. I wrote of the Battle of Guadalajara, where an Italian expeditionary force was routed in March 1937, as "one of the twelve of fifteen decisive battles of history." It makes me feel foolish to see that in cold print in a book today, when everyone has forgotten Guadalajara. But I may not have been entirely foolish. After all, it was the first decisive defeat of fascism in battle, the first time that free men had proved fascism's vulnerability. The Fascists went on to win the Spanish Civil War on behalf of Generalissimo Franco, and then, like the Imperial French of Napoleon's forces who had met defeat at Bailén in Spain, they were defeated in a much greater conflict.

It was at the last dramatic Cortes of the Second Spanish Republic in the Castle of Figueras on February 1, 1939, that

Negrín said: "Countries do not live only by victories, but by the examples which their people have known how to give in tragic times." Spaniards who were there and those who know will never let the memory of Figueras die; and when some day there are free Cortes again in Spain, they will stem proudly from that brave meeting in the cellars of an old castle in Catalonia.

Had Premier Negrín and the Popular Front, with its predominant Socialists and Republicans, won, Spain, I am still convinced, would not have gone Communist. That was one of the mistakes the democracies made. If Britain and France had fought at Munich-time in 1938, while the Spanish Civil War was still on, they would have had Republican Spain at their side, a democratic Spain in our sense of the word. Instead, the Allies (including the United States) had to contend with a hostile Spain that maintained a formal neutrality but helped the Axis.

It is too soon for history to pass a final judgment. I am not pretending that my opinion or that of any contemporary can be final. We see clearer today than we did eighteen or twenty years ago; but to take its rightful place in history, the account must be set down by a later generation, by those who write after passions are spent, who were not seared in the Civil War's fire or blinded by prejudices.

As a war it was lost by democracy, won by reaction. Those who fought for freedom lost in terms of men, materials, territory and power. As a page of Spanish and world history it had a brightness that can never be lost, although that brightness seems hopelessly dimmed—and even denied—by so many Spaniards today.

"The war in Spain," wrote Ciano, "which had ended with the complete defeat of those who had so often declared their certainty of conquering Fascism, signalized the collapse of the Bolshevik movement in Europe."

The irony of it! Here we all are in the year 1957 with Italian Fascism a sordid memory and with Bolshevism triumphant, while a Caudillo still sits uneasily on a lid in Spain.

There was only one thing that could be safely predicted in those days. Back in 1937, as with many others who were in the midst of events, it was easy for me to call attention to the similarity of the Japanese aggression in China and the Nazi-Fascist aggressions and to make the obvious prediction that the lines would meet.

"The youth of the world is going to war," I wrote, "one in Africa, one in Europe, one in Asia, and who shall say there are not more to come? You who stroll along the 'Great White Way' thinking complacently how far away it all is from peaceful America—you, too, will feel a tap on your shoulder one of these days, and will hear the call."

We have learned some lessons since Spain. Korea was wonderful proof of that. In a sense Spain was a sacrifice, but it cannot be said that it was fought in vain. It was part of the world struggle against totalitarianism, fought at a time when one of the Janus-faces of totalitarianism was turned our way, as it was in World War II. The issues were somewhat confused, in Spain, but it is true to say that one evil was fought there for the first time. We should not forget that until September, 1939, only one people and one-half of a country fought fascism.

That was the negative side, but the Civil War was, too, in its way, a fight for liberty and democracy. As such, in a material sense, it was lost; but it can await with confidence the verdict of history.

"Countries do not live only by victories. . . ."

iii.

THE WORLD WAR

THE SPANISH CIVIL WAR ENDED ON APRIL 1, 1939; THE Second World War began on September 3, 1939. For Spain, the first was a cataclysm, the second merely a great storm on the horizon. The Spaniards felt the beat of the winds and rain and heard the roll of the thunder, but the storm spent itself elsewhere. For that they had Generalissimo Franco to thank. It was to be his greatest contribution to the nation over which he is still ruling.

There is an irony in this which was symbolized by the fact that Generalissimo Franco started the World War with two huge, autographed photos on his desk, one of Hitler and the other of Mussolini. He ended it with just one photograph— that of Pope Pius XII.

Those of us who had thought that the Germans and Italians had come to stay, or that Franco Spain was to be dominated by them were wrong. In the five months between the wars the Nazi and Fascist troops got out. The Germans were left with considerable commercial and trading influence and with the high regard of General Franco and his advisers.

The Italians were left with nothing but the contempt and derision of the Spaniards and a huge credit which was never repaid.

Spain was prostrate, but except for the diehards who had dwindled fast or been driven into France, she was overwhelmed with relief. The philosophy that "anything was better than another civil war" became the main strength of the Franco regime—and continues to be so. As is often the case when revolutions or wars are lost, the losers quarreled in their bitterness among themselves. There was an ignoble scramble for a small part of the Government's treasure of gold reserves. By far the greatest part went to Moscow, where it remains to this day; some went to France and was promptly turned over to Franco.

The last Premier, Don Juan Negrín, suffered the bitterest reproaches. It was his courage and will power alone that had kept the war going in the last months. He had realized that if he could only hold out long enough, the greater conflict would come along and save Republican Spain. His calculation was not far off, but "a miss is as good as a mile." He and Loyalist Spain lost, and the price that had to be paid, particularly in Catalonia where the resistance went on right up to the French border, was high.

Although the Loyalists broke up in quarrels and recriminations, Dr. Negrín always considered himself the legitimate leader of Republican Spain. After all, he was the last Premier and he did not resign, nor was he overthrown by the Cortes in Spain. He considered it his right to live as well as act in the style of the head of a government. Therefore, he kept an undetermined amount of Government money for himself. For this he was bitterly condemned by other Republican exiles who felt that this money—or much of it—should have been used to relieve the distress of refugees in France or Mexico.

Dr. Negrín kept a dignified silence. He wrote his memoirs, but stipulated that they were to be published only after his death, which occurred last autumn on November 12, 1956. Those, like myself, who had watched him closely during the Civil War and who retained a deep admiration and affection for him in the after years, will have no doubts about the verdict of time. He lost, but he made a mark on Spanish history of which future generations will have reason to be proud. No one better than himself realized what bad mistakes he had made, but history does not count mistakes only. He was a great Spaniard, and he fought for all that was best in the contemporary aspirations of Spain. The battle he lost will be resumed, and because he fought it so well, it can be resumed without civil strife—and sooner or later it will be won. Those who fight for freedom never fight in vain.

In Spain after the Civil War ended, there were weeks of terror as those who fought for the Loyalists or who supported them politically were imprisoned or executed. The Communists naturally suffered the most, for they had gone down fighting to the end. Communism was at the time the chief ideological target of General Franco and the Axis allies. To be sure, the Nazis and the Russian Communists were soon to make a pact and thus permit the Germans to start the Second World War, much to the embarrassment of the Franco regime. However, General Franco never wavered in his anti-communism and ultimately found himself back at Hitler's side, even to the extent of providing a "Blue Division" of Spanish troops to fight against the Russians on the Eastern front.

The censorship in Spain, the previous record of the Insurgent forces and the natural fears of the exiles and of pro-Loyalist foreigners everywhere led to exaggerated accounts of the reprisals being taken by the Franco Government. We will never know how many men and women the Nationalists executed during and after the war, for they naturally kept no record. We do know about the Loyalist executions, for the Franco government, after the Civil War, collected all the names it could get of persons executed by the Republicans. The accounting was registered in the National Sanctuary at Valladolid. The total is 54,594; in addition, 7,299 religious were shot—12 bishops, 283 nuns, 4,266 priests, 2,489 monks and 249 novitiates. These figures are, of course, terrible; but it is worth noting that they are far, far below the popularly accepted figures, and they are hardly likely to be an underestimation.

The fact that the Rebel forces gradually conquered more and more territory as the war progressed, executing as they went along, plus the reprisals taken after the final collapse, makes it seem evident that they killed many more Spaniards than the Loyalists. However, this can never be proved.

An idea of the number arrested can be gleaned from the fact that in 1941, more than two years after the fighting ended, there were 241,000 political prisoners. Amnesties gradually reduced the number, and for some years now, it is fair enough to say, there have been no political prisoners left from the Civil War. The total prison population nowadays is no more—or perhaps less—than it was before the Civil War, and the population has grown.

On my trips to Spain after the Civil War I got the impression that we really did exaggerate the toll that had been taken after the first summary wave of executions by the military. We have to remember the intensity of the passions aroused, the hatred that naturally vented itself in a last burst of fury, the conviction among the Nationalist leaders that the Loyalists were evil, treacherous men who deserved no mercy. The Spanish character does not forgive easily or quickly, and, as it happens, Francisco Franco has an exceptionally unforgiving nature.

Something like a quarter of a million Spanish men, women and children fled over the French frontier with what pitiful belongings they could take. This was one of the most moving "plebiscites" against fascist terrorism that has ever been seen. The French treated the refugees shamefully at the time, but at least they kept them there and gradually absorbed thousands into French life. A great many returned to Spain when amnesties were offered, but there are still more than 100,000 Spanish refugees in southern France, for the most part around Toulouse.

Thousands found their way to Latin America, especially Mexico, where they became useful adjuncts to their communities. A number of the leaders and a large group of children, sent by their parents, ended up in Russia. Hundreds of these returned to Spain just last year.

Wherever he was, life was hard for the Spaniard, and above all at home. The country was badly run. Being a typical military man, General Franco knew nothing about economics. When he froze prices at the 1936 level, he brought on a monstrous black market, the worst in Europe. A whole black market economy grew up. The middle classes—small businessmen, white collar workers, teachers, doctors, civil servants—all found themselves with insufficient income to live. They had to do two or more jobs, and many of them learned to live on the black market. For years it seemed as if the middle class was being eliminated and proletarianized, but it has been making a come back recently. However, the greater number still have to carry two or more jobs in order to live. That goes for Army officers, too.

Generalissimo Francisco Franco went serenely on. The difficulties of Spanish life never seemed to disconcert him, and they did not affect his position. People would tell you that Franco was a *buenissima persona*—a "very good man," but there were others around him who cheated. Franco, it was asserted, did not know that potatoes cost six pesetas a kilo, or whatever the price might have been, or that some ministers or Falangist officials were enriching themselves.

In other words, the Caudillo was being absolved from the mistakes of his Government—a process that we Americans have learned to understand in recent years. Franco had become the one great and towering figure of contemporary Spain and has remained the one and only such figure to this day. It has been an astonishing feat in the art of dictatorship, but then, Francisco Franco Bahamonde is an astonishing man.

One does not need to go into the subtleties of how much was intelligence, how much shrewdness and luck. These are parlor games, fascinating to discuss over cups of coffee but incapable of settlement. Franco's career could also provide an absorbing study in the extent to which the leader dominates events or events control his actions. The ascertainable, obvious facts are fascinating enough, and they reveal Franco's character. A Caudillo of Spain does not live in a goldfish bowl like a President of the United States; but he cannot live like a hermit, either.

The character, either pro or con, that was built in the public mind during the Spanish Civil War made little sense. To his champions in the United States, for instance, Franco was a paladin of Christianity, a crusader, the *"parfit gentil knight,"* leading the armies of righteousness against the powers of darkness. Such Americans would hear—or believe—nothing wrong of him. This picture has lingered through the years and partly explains why, when General Franco is criticized in organs like *The New York Times,* the Editor receives indignant letters from a certain number of Catholic readers or from those to whom anti-communism is the sum total of wisdom. It was and is, of course, a greatly distorted picture.

So is its opposite, that of a stupid, weak, cruel and perfidious general who had sold his nation to the Nazis and Fascists. The character of Franco, as we shall see, is curiously un-Spanish, but he was and is, nevertheless, the exemplar and leader of certain profoundly Spanish forces. No one who really knows anything about him today can doubt the depth and sincerity of his convictions. One might say that he was tragically wrong; a case could be made, from a partisan point of view, that he was evil. And certainly he was cruel—his conduct of the war and its aftermath are sufficient proof of that.

However, there is a cruel streak in many Spaniards, and the whole Civil War, on both sides, was a demonstration of that. Passions ran high and convictions of evil—again on both sides—were deep. The Spaniard does not rate either his own or other people's lives as highly as we do, and a military man, especially, was less likely to count the cost in lives and property of a military campaign than a civilian-led government. The bombings by German and Italian planes of Spanish cities—Guernica and the blitz of Barcelona in March 1938, were examples—aroused the horror of Spaniards and foreigners; but to a general they would be necessary, if regrettable, concomitants of a campaign in which victory, and not the cost of victory, was the primary consideration. In other words, in this respect Franco was no more cruel than the allied generals who directed the bombing of German cities later on.

I did not find, on my recent trips, that Spaniards on the whole harbored any lasting resentment against the Caudillo for the manner in which he fought his war. This was not the case in the American Civil War where, for instance, General Sherman's march through Georgia is still resented almost a century afterward. Of course, those families who were the victims of unnecessary cruelty are not likely to forget or forgive so easily. But the Spaniard is tough and philosophical; he would expect a war to be fought without quarter, and in some respects the Republicans fought their war the same way.

Vae victis—let the conquered beware—is one of the oldest cries to echo through history. The Republicans had lost, and they had to pay the price. Francisco Franco was no Abraham Lincoln, either as a man or as a statesman. It was not in his character to try to heal the wounds of the war or to unite the warring sides by generosity and magnanimity. The sort of justice that is tempered by mercy does not come naturally to him. He was, in time, to make concessions and to permit his people to demonstrate their own sense of kindness and comradeship so that today we see the old wounds healed or healing. But in the early years after the Civil War justice was stern.

General Franco, in any event, felt impelled to establish his regime on the two pillars to which he never ceases calling attention—discipline and unity. This is the military character at work. The Civil War was brought on, to a considerable extent, because generals like Franco could not stand the hurly-burly, untidy, almost chaotic state of affairs under the Second Republic. For their type of mentality, law and order are ends in themselves, the greatest of all civic virtues, far more necessary than liberty, and, in fact, impossible in a regime of freedom. This is one of the basic goals of all variations of fascism, as it is of all military dictatorships.

General Franco ended the Civil War with his authority unchallenged by any men or any elements of Spanish society. His position was unassailable. He could have made many civic, political and educational concessions easily and safely. However, that would have been completely out of character. He does not believe in the things that would happen after liberties are restored. The result would be messy, and might get into intellectual fields that would be disturbing to him and to the Church. The people are to be treated well, taken care of, guarded, helped; but the idea that they should have a civic existence of their own is as foreign to Franco's mentality as it would be to let the rank and file of his regiments do as they please. The Army is a hierarchical structure in which orders are transmitted downward from himself as Commander-in-Chief to rank after rank in due order. Discipline and unity—and the State must be run similarly insofar as it is possible.

General Franco's chances of establishing discipline and unity did not seem promising in the long run, since few races are more undisciplined than the Spanish and the regional forces would never cease their centrifugal pull. However, Franco was helped by two overriding factors which obtain to this day: the prostration from which the nation and people had to recover and the feeling that anything was better than to risk another civil war.

What Franco had to do was to clamp a lid down—or a number of lids—and sit on them. This solved nothing, but it helped to maintain "law and order," which provided bene-

fits to the community and also permitted Francisco Franco
to stay in power.

The situation in Catalonia was typical of how Madrid's
central authority was maintained at the price of suppressing,
for the time being, Catalan nationalism. A similar picture
could be drawn of the Basque country. These are the two
regions which stand out because of their distinctive race,
culture, language, customs, character and history.

Catalonia is the most progressive, economically rich and
cosmopolitan region of Spain. The Catalan looks down on
the Madrileño, whom he feels he is supporting by his industry,
and whose narrow religiosity, arrogance and monopoly of
the administration he resents. The Catalan is by nature, and
for practical reasons, in the political opposition to any central
government in Madrid. Since a military dictatorship like
Franco's does not brook opposition, it was and is necessary to
hold Catalonia down.

The process has unquestionably earned the enduring hostility of the Catalans (as a similar process aroused the antagonism of the Basques). There has been an absolute ban on
the teaching of the Catalan language in all primary and
secondary schools. For nearly ten years Catalan could hardly
be spoken in public. It cannot be used as an official language.
All Catalan periodicals were suppressed and, except for the
classics, the Catalan language was banned in books, theatres,
cinema and on the radio. In recent years, however, a Catalan
theatre has been permitted in Barcelona.

Catalans believe there has been a deliberate weakening of
their industries, especially textiles. However, when it comes
to business acumen, the Madrileño is a child compared to the
Catalan, who is an expert at tax dodging, double entry book-
keeping, bribery, exchange manipulation and the like.

The important aspects to keep in mind are, first, that the Catalans resent very much what Franco has done to them and, secondly, that they have been able to do nothing about it. Perhaps one should add that, in reality, they have not wanted to do anything about it for the simple reason that this would have meant revolt and all its attendant strife and chaos. The Catalan industrialists, for instance, had their factories taken away from them by the Loyalists—often Anarcho-Syndicalists—in the Civil War; General Franco, at least, gave the factories back and has prevented another attempt at a social revolution.

There is a constantly heard story in Barcelona about the Catalan who raved bitterly against Franco. When his tirade is finished, his friend says: "Yes, I understand, you are right. And whom would you like to have in power now?" "Why, Franco, of course," the complainant answers.

An extraordinary apathy had settled over the Spanish people like a pall. It was extraordinary because the Spaniards are the least apathetic of people.

The Generalissimo and his supporters set about creating —or perpetuating—a myth, that Franco and the Nationalists had saved Spain from communism. The Civil War was renamed "The War of Liberation." The Loyalists were never referred to as anything but *los Rojos*—the Reds. It is extraodinary nowadays to hear even Spaniards who were sympathetic to the Republic speak naturally, and without attaching any special meaning to the label, of *los Rojos*. The generation that has grown up since the Civil War never thinks in any other terms. It is just about the most successful application of a "publicity stunt" that I have ever come across in my life.

In those first years after the Civil War, Franco had far more to do than just to sit on the lid of a Spain which, in any event, was prostrate and licking its wounds. Neither the nation nor the shell-shocked people wanted any new adventures. General Franco did not need to feel the pulse of his people to realize that. Once the Second World War began his problem was to hope and pray for an Axis victory and to do what he could to bring it to pass, but to keep out of the war and to keep the war out of Spain. Later came the problem of adjusting himself to the forthcoming allied victory which he had wanted to prevent.

The true measure of the man's character and capabilities was shown in this extraordinary feat of double-dealing. The Spanish people will always be enormously grateful to him for succeeding. In one vital sense, so were we and the British. There is no question that the war in Europe and North Africa would have been far more difficult for the Allies if Franco Spain had become a belligerent on the Axis side.

Hitler and Mussolini had been given every reason to believe that the Franco regime would become an open ally from the beginning. However, Franco was much too canny to make the mistake that Il Duce made. Mussolini carried Italy into the war—the infamous "stab in the back"—when Germany overran France in May and June 1940. Italy paid a terrible price, materially and in the eyes of the world, for that miscalculation. Franco staked out his claim, but had sense enough to wait.

"At a time when, under your guidance," he wrote to Hitler on June 3, 1940, "the German Armies are bringing to a victorious conclusion the greatest battle of history, I would like to offer you the expression of my enthusiasm and admiration, as well as those of my people, who have been following with great emotion the glorious prosecution of a fight which they feel to be their own, and who realize the hopes that were kindled in Spain already in the days when your soldiers were fighting side by side with ours in a war against the same, though hidden enemies.

"I need hardly assure you that it is my sincere desire not to stand aloof from the matters which preoccupy you and that I would be deeply gratified to render you, at any time, such services as you might consider most valuable."

During that same month of June 1940, in a breach of the international statute, Spanish troops seized Tangier and five months later it was formally annexed. By stationing a large army in Spanish Morocco, Franco forced many Allied troops to be immobilized in North Africa. In June 1941, the Generalissimo organized the "Blue Division," which fought as the 250th Division with the German armies against the Russians from October 1941 until November 1943. Even afterward, so-called Spanish volunteers stayed and fought with the Germans against the Russians.

The documentation on Franco's aid to the Axis and on his pro-Axis sentiments is long, numerous and impressive, but certainly one-sided, for Franco was playing on both sides of the field. A few high spots are being mentioned here because it is important to realize why the United Nations ostracized Franco Spain for about five years after World War II. The basic, hostile documentation is summarized in the American White Book, "The Spanish Government and the Axis," March 1946, and above all in the "Report of the Sub-Committee on the Spanish Question" of the United Nations Security Council, published in June 1946.

General Franco had written Mussolini on August 16, 1940, that "Since the beginning of the present conflict, it has been our intention to make the greatest efforts in our preparations, in order to enter the war at a favorable opportunity." However, the Germans were of two minds about Spanish intervention. There was a famous conference between Hitler and Franco in the Fuehrer's railway car at Hendaye, on the French border, on October 23, 1940, during which the Fuehrer tried for ten hours to persuade the Caudillo to become a belligerent and to allow German troops and arms to cross Spain and attack Gibraltar. At the end Hitler is supposed to have been so furious and frustrated that he jumped up and down in one of his noted screaming fits. Franco, one may be sure, was as cool as a cucumber.

All the same, as the documents show, the German and Spanish General Staffs did work out a joint plan for the capture of Gibraltar and the expansion of Spanish territories in Africa. Spanish and German troops even trained for the assault on Gibraltar, and a date—January 10, 1941—was set. However, it never came off, perhaps because Hitler was by then absorbed in preparations to attack Russia, or, more likely, because Franco never intended to go through with it.

Where Franco was of most help to the Germans and Italians was in such fields as providing submarine bases and ports for fueling warships, airbases for the Luftwaffe, and spying on British and French ship movements for the Axis, especially through the Straits of Gibraltar. Viscount Templewood, who as Sir Samuel Hoare was British Ambassador in Madrid during the Second World War, wrote in his memoirs that "On both the African and European coasts, there was a chain of radio stations to report direct to Berlin the movements of Allied shipping."

However, in the last year of the war, Franco helped us in similar ways. We Americans had some special reasons for complaint from the moment, on December 8, 1941, that the Spanish Minister of Foreign Affairs sent congratulations to the Japanese Legation on the successful attack against Pearl Harbor. Toward the end of the war, on March 10, 1945, President Roosevelt wrote Norman Armour, then our Ambassador in Madrid, a letter in which he said that the Franco Government "had been openly hostile to the United States and had tried to spread its Fascist party ideas in the Western Hemisphere."

"These memories [of Spain's aid to the Axis]," Mr. Roosevelt continued, "cannot be wiped out by actions more favorable to us now that we are about to achieve our goal of complete victory over those enemies of ours with whom the present Spanish regime identified itself in the past spiritually and by its public expressions and acts."

However, for many Americans the attitude and actions of Franco in World War II were easily "wiped out" or excused and explained. One of the outstanding apologists for the Caudillo in the United States was Professor Carlton J. H. Hayes of Columbia University, who had been a historian of note and who became American Ambassador to Madrid in the World War from 1942 until 1945. In a volume published in 1951, called *The United States and Spain*, he said: "There is no doubt in my mind that General Franco and his Government were determined from the beginning of the World War to stay out of it if at all possible."

"Spain did not intern any of the 1,200 American airmen who force-landed in the country, but gave them refuge and permitted them to leave," he went on to say. "It did the same with 30,000 Frenchmen and sizable groups of Poles and Netherlanders who passed through the country on their way to join the Allied armies. By special agreement in 1944 it provided us with important air bases, first for our commercial planes, and then for our military planes. Also, early in 1944, in compliance with our request, it recalled the Blue Division. And from within Spain, we were enabled, through our intelligence services—Army, Navy, and O.S.S.—to organize and conduct in German-occupied France the espionage which contributed immeasurably to the success of our Normandy campaign."

Professor Hayes had previously written a book, called *Wartime Mission in Spain,* in which he explained and documented this belief at great length.

Allied statesmen indulged in private criticisms and public acknowledgments, for it was a mixed picture, but once the war ended the criticism was outspoken and virtually unanimous. The picture then drawn was a completely black one, which was hardly fair, for there had been bright spots. After all, Peronist Argentina which was as bad as Franco Spain, and even worse in some ways, was admitted to the United Nations, while Spain was insulted and rejected.

The procedure had a great effect on Spain but quite the opposite from what the democracies and the Soviet bloc intended. It helped and strengthened General Franco. If he is in power today it is certainly in part due to the way clumsy and shortsighted attacks from abroad led all Spaniards, whatever they thought of him, to rally round the Caudillo.

At the San Francisco Conference to launch the United Nations in April 1945, a resolution was passed barring "nations whose regimes have been established with the aid of armed forces of countries that have fought against the United Nations, as long as those regimes continue in power."

The following year the Sub-Committee on the Spanish Question of the Security Council reached the conclusion that: "In origin, nature, structure and general conduct, the Franco regime is a Fascist regime patterned on, and established largely as a result of aid received from Hitler's Nazi Germany and Mussolini's Fascist Italy."

That dotted the "i's" and crossed the "t's." On August 2, 1945, at Potsdam, Truman, Attlee and Stalin had said that they would not favor Spain for membership in the United Nations, and in March 1946, the Big Three—the United States, Britain and France—actually called for the overthrow of the Franco Government. Then on April 29, 1946, a Security Council resolution was passed referring to the "unanimous moral condemnation of the Franco regime in the Security Council." Finally, in December 1946 the General Assembly of the United Nations passed a resolution urging member nations to withdraw their Ambassadors from Madrid. At the same time Spain was barred from the affiliated agencies of the United Nations and from United Nations conferences.

It was utter folly. The United States lost the services in Spain of one of our best diplomats, Ambassador Norman Armour, who would have been able to help the cause of democracy in Madrid. We even barred Spain from Marshall Plan aid although we had offered it to the Soviet Union. The idea that we could help overthrow Franco by starving the Spaniards and depriving them of jobs was completely foolish.

Of course, it had the opposite effect. The Franco regime was strengthened. The blows we struck hurt Spanish pride. They forced people to say, in effect: "We are Spaniards and we will settle our own affairs, but we are not going to accept insults from foreigners."

It goes without saying that Generalissimo Franco was not shaken for one second in the utter assurance of his righteousness. In fact, it is more than probable that he has never been shaken in that respect in his life. The Spaniard, at best, is fairly impervious to criticism because he is so sure that the foreigner does not and cannot understand him. The Spanish feeling of superiority toward foreigners, at least in the abstract has been noted by all travellers who study Spain. This is not a personal attitude, for the foreigner is treated with the utmost kindness and cordiality; it is a general attitude.

It would never occur to General Franco that he could be wrong or that he could have done something bad or reprehensible. He is completely protected by an overwhelming sense of self-righteousness. This is not an unusual trait in absolute dictators of any race or time; it is, in fact, a necessary part of the mechanism that keeps them going.

At any rate, how could General Franco be convinced that he was wrong in his posture when the whole free world, at least, has changed its attitude and accepted Spain back into the comity of nations with cordiality? Franco did not change his politics in the slightest; we all changed ours.

It took several years. Ambassadors started dribbling back to Madrid. Economic relations were strengthened. Finally, in November 1950, the U.N. General Assembly passed a resolution to revoke the recommendations for the withdrawal of Ambassadors from Madrid and barring Spain from membership in international agencies of the United Nations.

To be sure, the preamble of the resolution carefully said: "The establishment of diplomatic relations and the exchange of Ambassadors and Ministers with a Government does not imply any judgment upon the domestic policy of that Government."

This was not going to worry the Caudillo. If the rest of the world was so misguided as not to appreciate the virtues of the Franco regime, that was its funeral. At the time General Franco made a speech in which he said: "It would be puerile for anybody to think we were going to change our ways, unless it was called for by our own convenience and in our own exclusive service." And to give him due credit, he had always made it plain that any improvement in relations with the United States and the United Nations would be no halfway meeting, but a question of meeting him on his own terms.

On July 16, 1951, Admiral Forrest Sherman, United States Chief of Naval Operations, had an interview with General-issimo Franco in which he brought up the possibility of an accord whereby the United States would establish air and naval bases in Spain. The mountain had moved to Mohammed.

iv.

FRANCISCO FRANCO

THE WORLD SCENE, AT ANY GIVEN TIME, IS STUDDED WITH figures who are the protagonists of the eternal drama of human history. Francisco Franco Bahamonde is, by any reckoning, a notable character on the contemporary stage. In those few years of the Civil War he was, indeed, a figure of worldwide importance. He had the power that makes for greatness, in a practical sense, and he aroused the passions of a divided public. As these passions, and the importance of Spain in the world picture, declined, so did the stature of General Franco. Yet it is not enough to say that he is a little man in a little country. He has played a great role in our time and he is an extraordinary character.

It was silly to think of him during the Civil War as a tool of the Germans and Italians. Francisco Franco was never anybody's tool. It was equally foolish to think of him in the past decade as the servant of forces like the Church, Army, Falange and big business. Franco has been nobody's servant.

No one today is going to stand back in complete objectivity and draw a picture of Francisco Franco as impartial history is finally going to see him. We do not have the material to construct such a picture and our vision is clouded by our feelings, whether these be favorable or unfavorable. What few biographies have been written of him are almost worthless, for they are apologias without balance.

It is not the events of Franco's life or what he did that need puzzle anyone, for these are well enough known. Future historians will not and cannot change the outlines. For our purposes, the very briefest account will suffice.

Franco was born at El Ferrol, near La Corunna in Galicia, which is the northwesternmost province of Spain, of middle-class stock, on December 4, 1892. His father was a naval paymaster, who reached the rank of General of Marines. The intensity and seriousness of Franco's character, as well as his ability, were shown by the fact that after graduating from the Military Academy in the Alcázar at Toledo, he became the youngest lieutenant in the Spanish Army. Then he successfully became the youngest captain, major and colonel.

Franco made his first mark in the ill-fated Spanish campaigns against the rebellious Riffs in Morocco. He there showed himself to be a man of intrepid courage—even to the point of rashness—and of stern discipline and devotion. He was always a man to be reckoned with, and one who could be trusted to carry out the limited objectives that officers normally face. He is generally credited with having drawn up the plans for the Spanish landing in the Bay of Alhucemas, Morocco, which was coordinated with the decisive French attack on land that ended in the defeat of Abd el Krim, the Riff leader.

It was also Franco, by now a general, who was entrusted by the then reactionary Republican Government with the repression of a revolt by the Asturian miners in 1934. It was a fierce working-class uprising with some atrocities on the part of the workers that were later punished with a cruelty and sadism that even the Civil War to come was not to match. The Government's commander was Francisco Franco, who brought Moorish troops into Spain for the first time in centuries and used them against Spaniards in the very region from which the Reconquest began.

Spain got a foretaste, in the Asturias, of what manner of man Franco was, but then, as now, he had his apologists. The Asturian miners were not only brutal and destructive, they were left-wing revolutionaries. The excesses used against them in repression caused a reaction that started Spanish communism on the road that was to give it some distinguished leaders and some popular support which it might otherwise have lacked.

What we are studying here is Franco's character; the interesting aspect of it displayed in the 1934 Asturian uprising was the simple, unadulterated philosophy of law and order, discipline and unity, which is the key to all the Caudillo's actions. A man so dedicated and with such firm convictions feels that it is necessary and right to use strong measures against lawlessness and, above all, against radicalism. Franco is the conservative, *par excellence*. If one sets an extremely high value on law and order, then it is not only legitimate but necessary to use stern and ruthless measures against those who disturb order. Franco was not only a hard man by character; his military career had inured him against the softer virtues of civilized life. The Moroccan campaigns were calculated to harden any character, for they were exceedingly cruel on both sides. Francisco Franco had been well endowed by nature to play a leading role in Moroccan events.

By 1936, the year of the revolt, he was not, by seniority,

the leading general, but when other generals—Sanjurjo and Mola, who were killed in plane crashes, and Goded, who was captured and executed in Barcelona—were eliminated, Francisco Franco had no rivals. It seems clear enough that in any circumstances Franco would have gone to the top. He is that kind of a man. He must stand alone unchallenged in authority, without partners, without confidants, without friends, without successors. So he has remained now for more than twenty years—*"Francisco Franco Caudillo de España por la G. de Dios"* as the legend on the 5-peseta coin now puts it. ("Francisco Franco, Caudillo of Spain, by the Grace of God").

It has been an extraordinary feat. As a technical exercise in the art of military dictatorship, no one can deny the "success" of this record. What few people seem to know, even inside Spain, since the censorship has always kept such things out of print, is what manner of man Franco is, his character, his way of life, his method of conducting affairs of state. Everyone knows who he is—that is the public record, and in discussing it we have already had some clues to his private life, which tells us what he is.

A lot of Spaniards will assure you that the secret (or one of the secrets) of his success is that he is un-Spanish. By that they imply that the average Spaniard is warm, impulsive, emotional, *simpatico*—which means having an attractive personality. Franco, they tell you, is none of these things. He is cold, hard, a block of ice, a snow man.

Certainly he is a man of oriental patience and iron self-control and these are not Spanish characteristics. It is nothing for him to make up his mind to a policy and keep it to himself for a year or two. It is not the alleged Spanish characteristic of *mañana* at work. It is not mental or physical laziness, nor is it indecision or weakness. It is patience, the ability to wait, to let time work, to dominate one's self; it is the excercise of will power.

One corollary is that nobody knows what he is going to do until he does it. All last year, for instance, discussions went on about constitutional changes but nobody could know what form they would take or whether, indeed, there would be any. General Franco is not only the absolute master in the Spanish house; he keeps his own counsel until the moment comes for him to give orders or to grant his consent. Like the paternal ruler he is, it gives him satisfaction, and it is also a valuable feature of his technique, to show his authority in settling "family" quarrels. Sometimes, as a matter of fact, he deliberately creates situations for temporary advantages in which the Falange and Army or the Church and Monarchists will quarrel with each other, and then he steps in.

The fact that he has no friends or confidants and does not share his power with anyone, naturally helps to make his Government policy unpredictable. His Ministers or the public may guess what he is going to do, based on what they know of him and on past performances, but it is always only a guess. This, obviously is a most effective source of power. Decisions come like lightning out of clear skies—no sooner said than done.

It has been my fate, as a journalist, to come in contact with many dictators, among them Mussolini, Hitler, Perón, Trujillo of the Dominican Republic, Somoza of Nicaragua, Pérez Jiménez of Venezuela. I can think of none who has that cold quality of Franco's. Within natural human limitations, one can say of the Caudillo that he has no nerves.

The best way to describe his self-control is to tell a story, a true story, of the days when he was a regimental

Colonel in the Spanish Foreign Legion in Morocco. He went away from his post for some days and received a call from the second in command, who told him that the men were protesting against the food they were getting and were refusing to answer bugle calls or report for the day's work. Their only answers were catcalls, boos and whistles. Colonel Franco listened coldly and merely told the officer to carry on. He finished the work he had to do and returned to the encampment.

The next morning, he turned out himself for roll-call, with the intention of inspecting the troops. When the bugle was sounded, nothing resulted but derisive cries from the barracks. He had the buglers sound again and again. The fifth time, the soldiers began straggling out; they lined up sloppily with their mess kits and other paraphernalia. Franco started his inspection.

Toward the middle of the line, he stopped in front of a great, hulking Legionnaire, who towered over the stocky little Colonel. The soldier said, "You like filth—well, here it is," and flung the messy food in his kit straight into Franco's face. It trickled down Franco's uniform and over his decorations. Any other Spanish officer would have taken out his revolver and shot the soldier dead on the spot. Franco's expression did not change. He took out his handkerchief, wiped his face and rubbed the mess off his uniform as well as he could, said nothing and went on. He had started to inspect the regiment and he was going to finish.

The job done, he dismissed the men, went to his office and called the officer in charge of the mess hall. "You will stay in your quarters for ninety days under arrest," he said to him, "but first I want you to give orders to improve the food immediately." Then he walked out, looked around, called an officer and pointed out the man who had thrown the food in his face.

"Take that soldier out," he said, "and execute him."

Such a man is, indeed, formidable. Franco's whole career, even as a youthful cadet, lieutenant and captain, has been like that. His promotions were in part a tribute to his bravery, but also to his machine-like application and his discipline. The normal Spaniard is the most undisciplined of men; Franco is as disciplined as a Prussian general. He has the classic military characteristics raised to an almost inhuman degree. Any army likes and needs martinets, as well as other types of officers, and such men are sure of promotion. Francisco Franco was bound to go far if his luck held out—and it has been phenomenal luck.

Yet, there is another side to his character. One might call it "the family man"—the husband, father and grandfather. There is also the "official man"—the charming, smiling Chief of State receiving visitors or appearing at public ceremonies. One must get these pictures to understand General Franco.

Every public official has his public manner. It is something he puts on like a coat. In Franco's case, it is like a uniform—strictly formal.

Franco is by no means inarticulate—not at all the "strong, silent man" type, although he can put on a stone wall of silence and maintain it with the obduracy and impassivity of an Oriental. It was this treatment of Hitler at periods in the Hendaye conference that drove the Fuehrer mad. In normal circumstances Franco talks a great deal, and his admirers insist that he is a brilliant conversationalist. From all accounts, however, it is usually more of a monologue than a conversation. He paces up and down the room talking; others listen.

In Lord Templewood's memoirs of his wartime ambassadorship in Madrid, he wrote of General Franco as "a family doctor with a good bedside manner." This was a clever characterization, by which the former Sir Samuel Hoare meant to convey the essential detachment of Franco from human relationship. A doctor puts on a manner. His basic attitude toward his patients has to be cold and scientific—otherwise he would not be a good doctor. What the patient sees is an attitude, a façade, an act that is being put on. This is true even when the character of the doctor is kindly and his relationship friendly—the act of treating a patient is itself artificial. This is what Lord Templewood intended to convey.

However, the real man is there, with General Franco as well as with the family doctor. Francisco Franco, "the human being," is best seen at his home near Madrid, going through a normal day as Chief of State. (His formal title is *Jefe de Estado*.) His house and office is the former sixteenth-century royal palace of El Pardo, fourteen miles northwest of Madrid toward the Sierra. It used to be occupied in the summer during the Monarchy, before the railroad linked San Sebastián on the northern coast to Madrid. After that it was rarely used. The last royal owner was the Prince of the Asturias, Alfonso, who had haemophilia and was killed in an automobile accident in Cuba in 1936.

When Franco decided to use El Pardo, he accompanied two Madrid architects there who suggested elaborate plans for enlargement, adornment and improvement. Franco listened in his customary silence and then merely said, "Be sure that all the windows and doors really shut." The Pardo Palace is more like a French chateau, beautifully kept, mostly white granite with pointed towers and steep, tiled roof, and with a formal garden in which, during the flower season, one will always see the Spanish coat of arms in flowers.

The grounds extend for miles back to the Guadarrama mountains and include an extensive forest full of oaks. Franco had it stocked with deer from another royal estate and he shoots them, not to mention partridge and rabbits. He is an ardent fisherman, as well, and his summers on the north coast are spent as much in fishing as in attending to affairs of state.

He built a swimming pool, tennis courts and a golf course at El Pardo, and added a little cottage away from the palace for quiet—his Petit Trianon. He played tennis until three or four years ago, but now that he is sixty-four and since he is on the heavy side, he has taken his doctor's advice and given up the game. He still plays golf now and then, but his chief sports remain hunting and fishing.

Although small and tending to corpulency, Franco is strong and vigorous. A few years ago he was unwell—some said prostate gland, some gall bladder—but whatever it was it has gone, and without the slightest publicity. Nothing could be more foreign to Franco's character or system of government than to take the public to his bedside as President Eisenhower did. At sixty-four anything can happen, but as of this writing Franco shows no sign of approaching old age or the flagging of his energies, and those who have been counting on the heavy hand of time or the definitive stroke from the Grim Reaper, would seem to have a long wait ahead of them. Franco can point to a grandfather who lived to 102 and another member of the family who died at ninety-eight.

The Generalissimo does not want to be awakened in the morning ever; he wants to wake up himself, which he generally does around 9 o'clock. He has breakfast—the customary slim, continental breakfast of coffee and rolls—in his rooms and reads the morning newspapers. This is something he has always insisted on; he wants no digests, although, since he only reads the Spanish newspapers, which are heavily censored and are extraordinarily insufficient, they can't be very illuminating.

At about 10, he goes to his office, which is in the Pardo. There he attends to his documents and sees Government officials until lunch time, which, in Spanish fashion, is well after 2 o'clock. He often lunches *en famille*, not only with his wife, but with his daughter and only child, Carmen, while Carmen's four children are available to play with in the apartment of the Pardo reserved for her family. His son-in-law, Dr. Cristóbal Martínez Bordiu, Marques de Villaverde, is a surgeon specializing in lung operations. When Dr. Bordiu first married Carmen in 1950, he used to spend a great deal of time at El Pardo, but it is an open secret that he and General Franco are now estranged.

The third of the four children is a boy and he has been given, legally, the name of Francisco Franco de Bordiu, so that he can carry on the name of his grandfather. Franco dotes on his grandchildren and plays with them whenever he can. They have an English nanny. Like many grandfathers he has a passion for taking photographs of the children, and he shows movies in the projection room at El Pardo to the two eldest.

Franco is fond of animated cartoons, especially those of Walt Disney. So enthusiastic was he about them at one time that he decided he would make one himself. This ambition was severely tempered when he learned how many hundreds of drawings are required. He never made one, therefore, but it was not for lack of technical ability. Like Churchill and Eisenhower, he is a devoted amateur painter and he has a genuine interest in art. As a young officer in Morocco he got into the habit of carefully sketching enemy landscapes and positions before an attack as a means of better visualizing the terrain in his tactical planning.

This does not mean that the Caudillo, any more than President Eisenhower, has a trained appreciation of art. He remains the amateur. Neither man is cultured and neither is an intellectual, but there is a vast difference in the two men's attitude toward "egg-heads." They are strange animals to Dwight Eisenhower, but he can take them or leave them. To Francisco Franco the intellectual is to be feared. Perhaps as Shakespeare's Caesar remarked of a contemporary intellectual, they "think too much."

No one will ever forget the historic ceremony held early in the Civil War at the University of Salamanca. Señora Franco was there, representing the Caudillo when General Millán Astray of the Foreign Legion joyously shouted: *"Viva la muerte! Abajo la inteligencia!"* (Hurrah for death! Down with intelligence!) The noted intellectual and philosopher, Professor Miguel de Unamuno, who was there, is said to have replied: *"Vencereis pero no convencereis"* (You will conquer but you will not convince).

That cry of "Down with intelligence!" has echoed through the years. In some ways it was symbolic. Certainly, Spanish culture is yet to recover from the blow delivered by the generals.

Franco's anti-liberalism and his positive anti-intellectualism are doubtless manifestations of his religiosity as well as of his militarism. They and culture are foreign to his mentality. He considers intellectuals useless appendages on the body politic at best, and a danger at worst, for to a man the intellectuals are anti-Franco. Not being a thinker, he has no sense

of philosophy or ideology. Hence, he could not hope to formu-
late even a pseudo-philosophy such as Mussolini helped to
evolve for the Fascisti. The best Franco could do was to accept in theory the philosophy which Falangism originally
borrowed from fascism and nazism and which has now
withered away.

But let us return to Franco's day. He takes no siestas, but
sometimes sits quietly on the verandah of the little house he
had built in the grounds of El Pardo and reads.

A Spanish "afternoon" of work starts at 5 or 6 o'clock and
goes on until at least 10, and that period, like the morning one,
normally is spent by Franco in his office. Then dinner. He
drinks little, taking no spirits and only one glass of wine with
each meal. He never smokes. About midnight, without fail,
he and his wife together kneel and say the rosary. Then he
reads in bed until 2 or 3 in the morning, either state papers or
books on world affairs and military history.

Wednesday is his receiving day for V.I.P.'s, Spanish and
foreign. Friday is Cabinet day. Until several years ago, Cabinet
meetings provided an extraordinary evidence of Franco's self-
control and his vanity. He sat at the head of a long table with
the other ministers. The conference would begin at 5 in the
afternoon and continue anywhere from five to eight hours.
Not once during any of those Cabinet meetings, year after
year, did Franco budge from his chair, however long the conference lasted. He did not, of course, require similar iron self-
discipline from his Ministers, who would get up, go out and
return. No smoking was allowed in the council room, but
Ministers could slip out for a cigarette.

This rigid and extraordinary weekly feat ended four or
five years ago. Cabinet meetings are now divided into two

sessions, one in the morning and one in the afternoon. Franco no longer sits immobile. This, like giving up tennis, is one of his few concessions to advancing years.

The Caudillo's character is bound to be complicated. How truly religious is General Franco, for instance? This is a question that Spaniards often ask themselves and often discuss. Those who knew Franco in his youth say he was not religious, and some even say he was anti-clerical. A famous Spanish phrase applied to Franco in those days was, *"Ni una copa, ni una mujer, ni una misa"* (No drink, no woman, no mass). Yet, from the time the Civil War began, he was the champion of the Church. The Spanish Church is stronger today than at any time in its history—which is saying a good deal. Youth is sometimes inclined to be less religious than middle or advanced age and there seems no reason to doubt the genuineness of Franco's religious feelings.

The subject is important because it has meant so much to Franco abroad and in retaining his power at home. His religiosity and his anti-communism are two characteristics that he and his followers have traded on.

It is no accident that in Spain one finds the extremes of ultra-devout Catholicism and atheistic anarchism. The Spanish character swings between those poles. It provides an intense fervor of worship and a fierce anti-clericalism at the same time. Each seems natural. Like love and hate, they lie closer together in the human heart than one might think from their manifestations.

The Spaniard has always been responsive to the idealistic appeal of religion. Once a leader or a movement is invested with a religious appeal, the chances of success are thereby enhanced. Any cause that raises the banner of Christ will win the average Spaniard. Franco was able to do this from the moment the Rebellion started in 1936. Coinciding, as the beginning of the war did, with the outburst of anti-clericalism on the Loyalist side, it placed the General naturally in the role of a crusader.

Franco's enemies have always suspected the genuineness and depth of his religious feelings. He displayed some traits in the Civil War that were far from Christian. In the end, these are matters of speculation and opinion; there is no way really of knowing. For instance, one can be impressed by the fact that the Generalissimo, according to popular belief, always keeps with him the silver-encased mummified hand of St. Theresa of Avila, which is one of the most precious religious relics in Spain. He "liberated" it during the Civil War and it seems to be like a talisman to him. However, there is nothing ostentatious about Franco's reverence for this relic, and it must be genuine.

On the other hand, many people are convinced that there has been a weakening of his moral fiber in these years of dictatorship and that, in a sense, shows a loss of religious feeling. Many years ago, when he commanded a machine-gun battalion in Morocco, the lieutenant in charge of the unit's accounts came out with a deficiency of 200 pesetas (about $30 or $35 at the time). All the officers talked about it at the club and the mess hall, saying, "Too bad for Blank. He'll have to make it up but it doesn't amount to much." When Franco learned of it, he ordered the lieutenant to appear before a military tribunal, and had him cashiered. Yet in these postwar years, as Chief of State, he has permitted some of his ministers and other officials to make millions for themselves in the black market or graft, and he turned his back.

It is partly the result of being raised on a pedestal—"beyond good and evil," one might say. This is a common position for all autocrats. They are not surrounded by the sort of men who tell them unpleasant truths or who dare to brave their wrath. A military man seems especially prone to this God-like complex. Franco's career has been based on hierarchy, on obedience to those above and from those below. At the top, in a military dictatorship, there is no one above to whom obedience is due.

There is only God, which is where one comes back to religion. A humble man who puts his trust in God could draw inspiration and simple virtues from his religious feelings; a proud man feels that God is on his side, that the decisions he makes must have providential guidance because he makes them. It is a variation of the "divine right of kings." The Dictator feels himself to have been divinely chosen as the instrument of Providence. For a Spaniard who is a Monarchist, as General Franco is, there is a traditional, almost instinctive conviction about God being on the side of the man whom He evidently chose to rule Spain.

One adulatory biographer claims that every night the Caudillo says a prayer before retiring that he composed for himself: "Lord, who entrusted Spain to my hands, do not deny me the grace of handing a Spain back to You which is truly Catholic."

As the Italians would put it, *"Se non è vero è ben trovato"* —(Even if it isn't true it ought to be). Note that it was the Lord who "entrusted Spain" to Franco, who will keep it in his personal possession and hand it back duly and truly Catholic. Is that being genuinely religious—or insufferably vain?

The Generalissimo's sincerity is not in question. He has always had the conviction that he was doing what was best for Spain and doing it for patriotic and—one must suppose—for religious reasons. He is as convinced as ever that Spain needs him and that, therefore, he must stay in power. Cynicism is not one of his qualities. He is a complicated character, but one that is built on some massive simplicities. An effective dictator needs an absolute assurance, an absence of doubt and self-question- ing, a faith in his destiny, a supreme conviction of righteous- ness. The Caudillo has all these things. They give him the solidity of a rock around which the stormy seas of events—even the events of these last eighteen years—beat in vain.

It has often been remarked that Franco has no friends and no confidants. In this he is like Hitler, Mussolini, Perón and innumerable other dictators. He dares not trust any man, Spaniards will tell you, and that is why he has to put his trust in God. As Article 47 of the Statutes of the Falange puts it: "The Chief of State answers to God and to History."

Another paradox of his character is that for all his aloofness from the people, he wants them to be taken care of, materially speaking. At least, he has an intense interest in all the social services, which are extensive and which he has fostered. This is true despite his lack of interest in and technical ignorance of economic affairs—which is the mark of all modern dictators. His concern with the social services is a reflection of his military paternalism. He wants to further the material well-being of his "soldiers"—the people of Spain.

Franco does not seek publicity or applause, being in this respect more like Salazar of Portugal than like Hitler, Musso- lini or Perón. There is no public hysteria as with Hitler; no effervescence, as with Mussolini. Franco wants obedience, not adulation or flattery. One goes to the biggest bookshop in Madrid to ask for a biography of the General and the answer is that the only one in recent years is out of print and that someone is preparing a new biography.

He seeks no hero worship in the way Hitler and Mussolini

did. For them, the cheers of the crowd were like heady wine; for Franco, they would be something to accept dutifully.

The last dictator to rule Spain before Franco, General Miguel Primo de Rivera (1923-1930) was popular. The urge to liberty was against him and he was finally driven out, but he was *simpatico*—the people liked him. When General Franco appears in public he is applauded very politely by whatever crowd happens to gather. There is neither warmth or animosity.

The Generalissimo went to Seville last year for the Feria, the Easter celebrations, and he went out of his way to curry favor, which was unusual for him. It was the time of the strikes in the north and he was worried. However, Sevillans told me that there was no popular warmth for him whatever. As he drove along the streets there would be mainly indifference and at best polite applause.

Franco is well guarded. The main task is entrusted to between thirty and forty tommy-gun bearing, red-beretted young soldiers, "The Generalissimo's Escort," who ride before and behind his car. Franco generally rides in a bullet-proof Rolls Royce. On parades and on special occasions he has his famous, colorful Moorish Guard on horseback—and always there are plain clothesmen scattered about. No serious attempt has been made on his life, so far as is known.

The Caudillo had his Moorish Guard with him in Seville, at the Alcázar, where he stayed. A Sevillan aristocrat I met (they are all rabid Monarchists) complained that Franco put on more airs than King Alfonso XIII used to do when he came to Seville and that he was less "democratic." Alfonso, it appears, was not guarded as closely as Franco, although there were a number of attempts on his life. Moreover, the King was generally sociable. On journies, he used to eat with his retinue and fraternize with them. Not Franco.

The result of all this is that the Caudillo has taken on a sort of impersonality. He is a fixture, an institution, from the popular viewpoint, not a man, and he arouses emotions only when Spaniards get together around a café table or at home and start talking about him. Then, the talk is invariably and openly anti-Franco. Yet, it is rare to hear words of hatred. Franco has achieved the extraordinary position of being, on the whole, neither hated nor loved in Spain. To those who know the Spaniards, this is the highest form of condemnation.

The Generalissimo's public life is modest, but no one doubts his importance, least of all himself. How else can one explain the extraordinary monument he has built to himself in death—the Valley of the Fallen, near the Escorial? It is referred to as "Franco's answer to Philip II" and, more frequently, as "Franco's Folly." The Caudillo is accused of having shown more interest and spent more time and thought in its construction than in the future of Spain.

As long ago as July 19, 1939, Count Ciano wrote in his report to Mussolini after a visit to Madrid that "There is more interest in rebuilding sanctuaries than in reactivating the railroad service, which is still in a very bad state." It is hardly unfair to repeat that sentence today.

Whenever the tomb is mentioned people laugh or throw up their hands in dismay. It has cost vast sums—no one knows or can ever know how much, for some of the money must have come from the budget, although most was from public and private "contributions." The labor in the early years was "redemption through work" and hence a disguised cost.

The sanctuary stands just about where the Rebel columns coming down from the North at the beginning of the Civil War were stopped in the Guadarramas and held for the remainder of the war. It is essentially a stupendous tomb that is without parallel in any country in modern times. So far as all Spaniards are concerned, it is General Franco's tomb. I was given permission to visit it and the very imposing and costly monastery behind the sanctuary, which is still empty, although it has been completed.

In the last year or two it was decided to call the sanctuary the Valley of the Fallen. It lies in a high valley in the Guadarrama Mountains about thirty-two miles from Madrid by road and only four miles from the great, grim mass of the Escorial, where Philip II "built a cell for himself and a palace for God." Some Spaniards go so far as to say that nothing comparable to the Valley of the Fallen has been built since Cheops constructed his Pyramid. It originally was conceived as a resting place for General Franco and a few important figures on the Nationalist side in the Civil War.

It was decided fairly early that the body of José Antonio Primo de Rivera, the Falange founder, also would be buried there. José Antonio's body now rests before the altar in the Church of the Escorial. It is also expected that some of the fallen on the Republican side will be buried in the sanctuary as a symbol that the hatreds aroused by the Civil War will likewise be buried.

The first and most striking feature of the Valley of the Fallen is the immense cross of granite that stands on the jumbled outcrop of solid rock in which the bodies will lie. The spot was chosen because when the cross is floodlit it can be seen from Madrid.

The cross is about 500 feet high. As with the Washington Monument, there is an elevator inside from which one steps on to the arms of the cross. At each corner of the bottom of the cross are statues of the Apostles in black marble of a porphyry type, each one more than sixty feet high. The base has even larger statues at its widened corners of the four cardinal virtues.

The sanctuary itself is called the Crypt, and that is just what it is. One walks through a great semicircular entrance adorned with many statues and high reliefs, through massive bronze doors into what really looks like the crypt of a church that would dwarf St. Peter's in Rome. It is more than 700 feet long, which is just about the length of St. Peter's Crypt.

One goes through a chancel door in heavy, very ornate bronze into a great vaulted corridor of the utmost simplicity. There is no color to be seen. Everything is gray granite and the effect is very gloomy. In this respect of oppressive, religious gloom, the Valley of the Fallen is like Philip II's Escorial and a world removed from an expression like the soaring, joyous religiosity of Chartres.

There are three shallow chapels on the sides, each dedicated to one of the Spanish Nationalist Army corps that fought in the Civil War. Over them will stand huge statues in alabaster marble.

As one gets up to the simple granite altar there is a sudden overwhelming burst of color and light, for the immense dome is one uninterrupted mosaic full of color and figures. A great figure of Christ dominates the center and all around are statues of many dozens of Spanish saints. It is, without question, one of the most splendid and beautiful mosaics constructed in modern times. From the altar to the top of the dome is about 500 feet—the same height as the Cross which stands on the outside, directly above. The conception is truly grandiose, which is why one has the right to place Francisco Franco, in this respect, alongside Cheops and Philip II.

There are two "pantheons," one on each side of the altar. Behind these pantheons, and running parallel to the main crypt, are great room-like niches where the bodies will be buried.

It may well be another year or two before all the statues and the other finishing touches have been made, but for practical purposes one can say that the sanctuary is as good as done. There is a lot more to it than the Cross and Crypt. A new, paved road had to be built up from the Madrid-Escorial highway. There is a lot of landscaping of the extensive grounds and a "Via Crucis," which will have the fourteen stations of the Cross in marble statuaries and columns from the entrance of the grounds up to the main monument.

But of the other things to be seen, the magnificent monastery and hospice, with its great chapel, is much the most impressive. It stands directly behind the Cross, to which it is connected by an underground passage. The original idea was that the Franciscan Order would take over the monastery and administer it and the sanctuary. However, it seems that the Franciscans, who above all others are devoted to poverty, flatly refused to place their monks in a setting of such luxury.

There are private baths and comfortable furniture in each cell and the basement contains electric ovens, dishwashers and driers, refrigerators and electric laundry equipment. The floors and walls are tile. A new dormitory at Harvard or Yale would certainly be less sumptuous and comfortable.

The Spaniards, who like all Latins take their religion with a dash of irony and raillery, have had their measure of amusement about Franco's monastery and about such touches as the bidets in rooms intended for visiting pilgrims. At any rate, I was told that the Benedictines, who in this respect are somewhat more worldly than the Franciscans, have agreed to administer the sanctuary.

Franco was extremely anxious to see the completion of

this massive work. If there were nothing else, this stupendous monument would give him enduring fame whatever future generations think of him and whatever disposition they make of the sanctuary. Few people in history have lived to construct anything so costly and colossal, something that will live for all time. That it should have been constructed by one man and essentially as a tomb for himself almost staggers the imagination. It is true that the concept was broadened, first to honor other Nationalist leaders and then to commemorate the "Fallen" on both sides in the Civil War, but for all Spaniards today, the sanctuary is Franco's tomb, first and foremost, and it may always be that.

It is *muy español*—very Spanish—to have a deep preoccupation with death, especially one's own. However, anyone like this writer who has watched Franco move around and bound up a stairway like a thirty-year-old must think that he has many more years to live.

Generalissimo Franco is not wearing himself out. He takes good care of himself, gets plenty of exercise and plenty of sleep, and is abstemious in his eating and drinking habits. Nothing is more risky or futile about Spain today than predictons. That includes Francisco Franco. The only sense in which his future seems assured lies in that incomparable tomb of the Valley of the Fallen. He, himself, wants it that way. But when, and under what circumstances? This is what no man can say.

$v.$

THE FRANCO REGIME

THERE WAS NO ALTERNATIVE TO GENERALISSIMO
Francisco Franco, and he has seen to it that none has arisen.
It is extremely unlikely that this situation will change while he
lives, although he is altering some of the forms of governmental
administration. The appearance may change even to the extent
of having a monarchy with a king once again; the substance
of power will lie in the hands of Francisco Franco, for he
cannot work, live with or conceive of any other status.

He has even been unable to loosen the reins of power,
which he could safely have done, for there was and is no one
to challenge his position. With his record in Morocco, his victory in the Civil War and his popular feat of keeping Spain out
of the Second World War, no rival could possibly present himself. As we can see now, all he had to fear was assassination,
not revolution. The Spanish people could not even bear the
thought of another civil war or anything like it.

If one had to seek a single reason why, eighteen years
after the Spanish Civil War, the same Caudillo is sitting on the
same lid in Spain, that is it. Franco likes to think of the position

as a pyramid with himself as the point, but in reality he has never had such popular support as that figure would imply. The average Spaniard was in a classic position—he could not live with Franco and he could not live without him.

Spaniards being what they are, the result is a paradox. The regime of Generalissimo Franco has never been more stable, and yet it could be overthrown in a few weeks. It could also last another few decades. This shows the extraordinary complexity of a situation that is perhaps as misunderstood abroad as anything comparable in the world. Those who are familiar with the thoughts and writings of Spanish exiles and political commentators abroad about the supposed weaknesses and approaching end of the Franco regime during his first two decades, or about a reign of police terror, or a totalitarian or Fascist state, get a shock on coming up against the reality today.

In the winter and spring of 1956, at the time of the university riots and even graver industrial strikes in the north of Spain, many outside Spain were saying: "This is the beginning of the end." In truth, there has been no element in the Spanish situation to suggest that the Franco regime is tottering or even weakening.

The country may be thought of today as existing on two planes. The surface is of a constantly, though slowly, improving economic well-being and of a civic peace that approaches apathy. Underneath there is a ferment of discontent and a desire for liberty that is growing every day. On top, all is tranquil because, as stated before, there is nothing to be seen but the Generalissimo sitting on a lid.

The whole situation can be summed up in a phrase: "This is Franco Spain." The regime is General Franco, who is strong and healthy at sixty-four years of age, and who is absolute master of all those elements of Spanish society and the state that are necessary in order to rule. No man, no group, no element has been permitted to threaten his power. This means that the end must come through an "act of God"—Franco's death or incapacitation—or through one of those popular explosions for which the Spanish people are so famous. Neither development is predictable. Spain today is like a keg of dynamite; there is no spark but it has plenty of explosive power.

To change the metaphor, what Franco did on achieving power over all Spain in 1939 was to turn the clock back. He even did more, for it is not much of an exaggeration to say that for a number of years he both turned the clock back and stopped it. Spain became static in a dynamic world, a stagnant backwash isolated from the great currents that were sweeping over the rest of Europe. What happened abroad meant little to Spain and what happened in Spain meant little or nothing to the rest of Europe.

The most talked of piece of writing in Madrid while I was there during a trip in April 1954, dealt with the hydrogen bomb whose power the United States had just demonstrated. The article treated the H-bomb humorously, and Madrileños thought it very funny.

Yet, Spain has been changing, and changing for the better. The two most important things happening in that country are the beginnings of an economic and social betterment, accompanied by the slow growth of a larger middle class, and, secondly, the gradual decline of Spanish isolationism from Europe and the rest of the world. The dictum that "Africa begins at the Pyrenees" is at last losing its sense.

Always, in governments of this type, wherever they are, one must take into account those who have a vested interest in the regime: the men of property who fear a civic upheaval, the men of the bureaucracy, high and low, who fear to lose their jobs or power, the professional politicians who are Franquist by definition, the Army, Navy and Air Force officers from the equivalent rank of colonel up, the clergy, who are especially favored. Add to these the great numbers of ordinary people who fear civil strife and above all another civil war, and the forces on which General Franco can count either to support or accept him become overwhelming.

The women alone would give him invaluable backing in a country like Spain, where the family is so powerful a social force. Women are a conservative element in any society, and in Latin countries they are also the religious element, listening to and obeying the priests. Since the Spanish Church is overwhelmingly pro-Franco, this has been a great source of support for the Caudillo.

Generally speaking, Spanish women have no interest in politics and never had any. They are educated by nuns, do not go to college, marry as soon as possible and want to have large families. The exemplary family life of Franco, and the religiosity that he and Señora Franco display, have a great appeal to the women.

Spanish women were never touched by the ideological or political aspects of the Civil War or its aftermath. They want their men to be able to live and work in peace; they do not care about forms of government, least of all about such ideological conceptions as democracy, freedom and liberalism. They simply do not want their husbands or sons to get into trouble, to go to jail and possibly to get killed.

Of course, in the poorest families where misery embitters the women too, there is a tendency to feel the way their husbands do about the Franco regime and all it stands for. However, the influence of the Church and the desire to see their men keep out of trouble, operate in favor of the status quo.

Franco has prevented another civil war; Franco kept Spain out of World War II; Franco represents peace and order—this is the way the women think.

And it must never be forgotten that few in any society are willing to risk imprisonment or death. Even during the Civil War I estimated that only about 20 per cent of the Spanish people—ten on each side—provided the driving force to keep it going. Hold a plebiscite anywhere and the people will vote for peace.

One of the surprises in Spain is to find that the almost universally accepted picture of the Caudillo's retaining his power by balancing against each other the Army, Falange, Church and big business interests is false. The Caudillo is much stronger than any or all of these factors taken together. Of these four elements only the Army and the Church really count, and they are not balanced against each other. The bankers and big business men are allowed much latitude in their fields, but are at the mercy of the bureaucratic state.

The Falange, Spain's only authorized political organization, is a shadow, a scarecrow that Franco picks up and shakes threateningly now and then. It has no power in itself. Its original Fascist doctrines have gone with the wind. Its present policies have no coherence or reality because the movement (it is not a party and does not claim to be one) is divided into many factions with many different ideas.

In theory, almost every adult Spaniard belongs to the Falange, which in itself makes it relatively meaningless. The vast bureaucracy is all Falangist as it was all Fascist in Mussolini's Italy; but that was not dedication to a movement, but a mere convenience. The entire labor union movement was "given" by General Franco to the Falange, but insofar as the Falange has any agreed philosophy of labor the top leaders concede that it is an ideal for the distant future. The Falange is dead on its feet, and it is surprising how many authorities admit it.

It can always be "re-activated" for specific times and purposes. It exists because it fills a real need. The Franco regime has no other political expression; hence any young man seeking a political career gravitates toward it. The local political bosses, in Spain as in all countries, control patronage, and they would be Falangists.

The only authorized syndical, or labor union, structure is Falangist, and since it has a role in wages and conditions of labor and since it does some collective bargaining for workers, it possesses power. The point being made here is that this power is delegated by Franco; it is in no sense the chosen form nor are these the chosen leaders of the workers. Some workers and peasants seem grateful that the Falange syndicates do often take their sides against the employers and landowners, but the vast majority despise the Falangists, whom they consider corrupt stooges of the ruling classes. If a dictator should emerge from its ranks with the support of the Army (an almost inconceivable development), he would still only be giving fictitious life to a movement that is simply a shell.

To be fair about Falangism, however, one should pay some tribute to the men who entered the movement and have stuck by its genuine ideals. There were many such in the early years and there are still some left. The founder, José Antonio Primo de Rivera, and many others, were young Spaniards of high patriotism, ideals and convictions. The movement degenerated, even during José Antonio's brief career, into fascist thuggery of the worst type, but those who lived and continued to struggle with the movement tried to keep a real philosophy of social radicalism. This element has been profoundly disappointed at the trends of recent years—bourgeois and monarch-ist—and they continually complain in some of the thirty-odd newspapers and half-dozen radio stations controlled by the Falangist movement.

However, the reactionary right-wing, Fascist-Nazi type of Falangism better suits the Caudillo's purposes and, on the whole, it has had the ascendancy over the years and has thoroughly discredited whatever good features the movement possesses. As a curious result, one finds elements of anti-Francoism in the Falange, anti-Monarchism and social progressivism. As another paradox, one finds the Falange somewhat infiltrated by the Communists. A number of Reds and Anarcho-Syndicalists found no difficulty in moving over at the end of the Civil War. It is never to be forgotten that the left and right wings of totalitarianism are very close to each other.

I do not mean to give the impression that the Falange is a totalitarian party or movement. It is nothing of the sort, since it has no such power as the Fascist party had in Italy, the Nazi party in Germany, or as the Communist parties have in the Soviet bloc today. The Falange has no power in itself; there is no political power outside the Generalissimo. There is no real armed militia, like the Italian Black Shirts, although the Falange can still turn out bands of armed thugs, as evidenced in the student riots last year. The Falangists have their similar uniform, Blue Shirts, but they only wear them for celebrations on special occasions.

Everything about the Falange shows its phony character. Only one student organization is permitted in the universities —the Falange "University Students Syndicate" (SEU)—but students join it or not as they please. Every Army officer from the rank of lieutenant up, by decree, is supposed to be a member of the Falange but, in fact, the military is quite hostile to the Falange. Priests can be Falangist, but just about none are.

So it goes. In the field of ideas and philosophy the Falange is equally nebulous. When it was Fascist, at least it was something; now it is nothing—ancient history, a figment of the imagination to which Franco gives spurious reality when it suits his purpose. He is "National Chief of the Movement," hence the Falangists cannot oppose his policies. What unity the movement has is imposed by the Generalissimo; in reality there are four or five warring currents. This is still another lid on which Franco sits; and when he goes, the Falange will almost certainly go with him.

The Army is completely under the Generalissimo's thumb, but it happens to be the only force in Spain, along with the police, that has the arms and ability to rule the country when the Caudillo goes. The generals are unlikely to do so for long, as they are, with honorable exceptions, reactionary, bigoted and upper-class. They have a typical military obsession for law and order at all costs.

The Army is a guerrilla force in Spain, not a fighting force in the normal sense, in that it is not equipped to fight a war. Its matériel is ancient, and the conscripts do not even have live ammunition with which to train. Spaniards make magnificent soldiers, as brave and hardy as any in the world, but to the highest officers and the regime the Army is essentially a political, not a military force.

Moreover, the officer corps has to spend from one-half to two-thirds of its time out of uniform as army pay is literally not enough to keep the men alive. They must do other work. The generals are socially and politically back in the nineteenth century, and no one of them has been allowed to become nationally popular or important. There is certainly a great deal of anti-Franco sentiment among the officers up to the equiva-lent of the rank of majors. Some day this antagonism may become important.

Meanwhile, the Army is the mainstay of the Franco re-gime. In so far as Franco has actual power, it lies in the Army and the gendarmerie. Without them, even he would fall; with them he is all-powerful.

The other great and powerful pillar of the Franco regime is the Roman Catholic Church. It has never held greater power in the history of Spain. However, it does not rule and will not do so, for Spain is obviously not going to become a theo-cracy. Let us simply note the importance of the Church at this point. The subject as a whole requires separate treatment.

The Franco Government functions like a cabinet system without a legislature that has any power, or a judiciary that can exercise impartial justice. Some persons also liken the system to a military staff with General Franco as the Com-mander-in-Chief and his Cabinet ministers as his *Estado Mayor,* or Chiefs of Staff. The ministers are responsible to the Gener-alissimo alone. If they are successful he keeps them; if things go wrong he takes no excuses and out they go. The Govern-ment, in a word, is not a governing body; it is a man—Fran-cisco Franco. Each Cabinet Minister is like an officer in charge of a division who carries on the day-to-day operations, but who is under the orders and control of the Commander-in-Chief, removable in one moment. It is a bit like the Ameri-can Cabinet system but the Caudillo, unlike our President, is not responsible to a legislature nor is there any division of powers. General Franco would no more allow the people to have authority than he would allow the privates and noncoms to say how the Spanish Army should be run. He always said that he was out to defeat what he called "nineteenth century liberalism."

Spain has been under a "State of War" since July 28, 1936, when the Defense Junta issued a decree to that effect. General Franco, as Chief of State, succeeded to the Junta as the sovereign power on October 1, 1936. By a statute of January 30, 1938, his decisions were given the force of law. Hence, he has unlimited power, all neatly bound in legal forms. Like all Latins, especially Spaniards, the Caudillo is a stickler for legality. To be sure, he sees to it that the laws give him what he desires, but he would be unhappy without those laws.

Franco Spain has a whole series of "basic laws" in place of a constitution. Among them are the Labor Charter of 1938, the Bill of Rights of 1945 and the Law of Succession of 1947. During most of 1956 a "Commission of 37," appointed by the Caudillo, worked to reduce these basic laws to two fundamental instruments, but nothing is being allowed to disturb the one factor that does not change—the character and power of Francisco Franco.

All political expression—socialism and Christian democracy, as well as communism and anarchism—is illegal. One of the commonest expressions you hear in Spain today is: "I don't mix in politics any more; there is nothing I can do about it." This does not prevent Spaniards from complaining to high heaven, loudly and freely. They have what Mussolini, in a classical allusion, called the *"jus murmurandi"* (the right to complain). This could never be stopped in either country, and both dictators realized that it is essentially harmless— even beneficial—as a means of letting off steam.

Of course, at any time and place in our modern era, political philosophies or aspirations take certain recognized forms. Parties and movements fit certain categories and have well-understood labels. It was the political Right that won the Spanish Civil War and the Left that lost. Consequently, democracy, liberalism, socialism, communism, anarcho-syndicalism all had to go underground. They all exist in a clandestine form, but they can have no leadership, no organization and no expression. Hence, every one of them is weak and the majority of the Spanish people must, in a formal sense, be apolitical.

We, who have been nourished on liberty, know that liberal democracy cannot and will not die, and we cherish the hope and belief that it will triumph over totalitarianism, whether communist or fascist. For all their faults, the Spanish Republicans who took part in the Revolution of 1931, who struggled to make a go of the Second Republic and who fought the brave and losing fight of the 1936-1939 Civil War, had a democratic philosophy. The country was not ripe for it, and they were even incapable of ruling by genuinely democratic means, but they were the expression of a profound and powerful political philosophy of freedom that came out of the "Generation of '98," and their work is far from dead; their fight was by no means in vain.

Dr. Negrín once said to me: "We Spaniards have a bias for liberty." So they have. I have already called attention to the curious way in which apparently isolated Spain gives a first expression to the great currents that are welling up through the tides of history. We Anglo-Saxons think of Magna Carta as the first great historic expression of political liberty. The restraints on their King by his subjects that the English won in 1215 had been achieved in Spain by 1188. The significant difference, of course, is that the English barons and burghers, and later the people, kept their liberties and expanded them. Spain has always had a "bias for liberty" and the courage to fight for it; the trouble has been the inability of the highly individualistic Spaniard to get together with other Spaniards afterward and apply the self-discipline and civic virtues necessary to make freedom and democracy work. And, besides, there was the fact that the Church and landowning aristocracy operated successfully in Spain to bolster the Monarchy against the people.

In this latter half of the twentieth century freedom cannot long be denied. The Spanish ruling class today has been clever in redefining and limiting "liberty" in such a way as to reach the paradoxical position that Spaniards now have liberty.

The most brilliant exponent of this thesis, judging from my conversations and reading, is Alberto Martín Artajo, Spain's leading Catholic layman, a former head of Catholic Action and a pupil of whom the Jesuits have every reason to be proud. He was Foreign Minister for eleven years until the Cabinet change of February 26, 1957. Martín Artajo begins from a probably valid thesis, that we must not judge Spain by United States standards. Many Spaniards have said that to me. I remember Juan Aparicio, Director General of the Press for the Franco regime, arguing that there is a basic difference of philosophy between our ideas and theirs, and it is no use arguing about it except for the pleasure of arguing; no result can be expected. It is true enough—and natural enough—that the Spanish mental and emotional processes are different than ours and different than the French, Germans and Italians. The foreigner is continually getting out of his depth. Things happen that baffle him; to a Spaniard they are natural.

So, a thinker like Martín Artajo argues that Spain is misunderstood; there is no comprehension of what is being attempted and what can be accomplished in the light of Spanish conditions and the Spanish temperament. "Spain," as he puts it, "is original."

The fear always expressed by Spaniards of this type is that liberty will turn to license. In its crudest and simplest form—and a most understandable one—it was put to me in this way by a Falangist leader who was a very young man in 1936: "You speak of liberty and the lack of it here. My father was a member of the highest tribunal of the Second Republic in Madrid, the equivalent of your Supreme Court. We are Basques; he was a conservative, and when the Civil War began he was taken out and shot. This is what happened when we had liberty, and we say we don't want any more of that kind of liberty."

The Foreign Minister put it on a more philosophic plane. He gave me a copy of a speech he made on June 16, 1951, in which his ideas were expressed.

"In good traditional and Christian doctrine," he said, "the liberties are of different grades. There are certain substantial liberties of a natural primary right, the birthright of human beings: that a man can worship his God, found a home, educate his children, work and go about with dignity and independence. These liberties, perhaps, are more secure in Spain than in any country in the world."

Such liberties, he went on to say, can turn to license, "that is, through the excesses of other liberties, such as press, political party, syndicate [trade union], strikes, which do not have the same nature or degree of importance because they are secondary, accessory liberties of an inferior order."

Hence, the Foreign Minister argues (and here speaks the subtle, Jesuitically-trained mind), "We Spaniards restrict our liberties somewhat, precisely because of our love of liberty."

Political liberties are, "from one viewpoint a luxury." The conclusion is that "Generalissimo Franco loves liberty, loves his freedoms as much and perhaps more than many others; but precisely because of this love of these holy liberties that were inherited from his ancestors, he takes care to protect them against the abuse of the enemies of liberty."

In other words, the theory that liberty is indivisible is decidedly not held by the rulers of Franco Spain.

Perhaps, to complete this picture, I ought to present a definition I heard a number of times from more simple-minded people. This comes from a chauffeur. (As is well known, journalists always speak to chauffeurs who, to be sure, are by no means always typical. However this was an oft-heard opinion and it is the down-to-earth expression of the philosophical subtleties of the upper, ruling class.)

"When I finish work, I can go and enjoy myself," the chauffeur said, "dance, or drink, or go to the cinema, or get drunk, and nobody will say or do anything to me so long as I don't insult other people."

Another way of putting it that I heard in different words was: "Give the people bread and bullfights [*pan y toros*, the equivalent of bread and circuses] and they will be happy."

In other words, "liberty" without freedom. Slaves can have that kind of "liberty" and often did have it in history. The Spanish character would have to change a great deal before Spaniards as a whole accept such a philosophy of life with any contentment.

A better expression of the Right-Wing, conservative type of political philosophy is taking form—a nebulous form as yet—in the growth of Christian Democracy. This is one of the common developments of the post-war era as we have seen it in France, Germany, Italy, Argentina and elsewhere. It cannot have an organizational strength and influence in Spain today because Franco allows no political expression of any form except Falangism. Through Falangism, politics go down the drain in present-day Spain. Moreover, there is an intellectual wing of the Christian Democratic movement that is anti-Franco. However, on the whole, it either is pro-Franco or has accommodated itself to Franquism—with an eye to the future. Since it can at least count on the benevolence of the Church today (and perhaps more later) it is a movement to keep in mind.

As a philosophy, it is similar to Christian Democratic movements in other countries. It has an extraordinary leader in Spain—Fernando Martín Sanchez Julia, an agrarian expert. Martín Artajo is considered to be intellectually in the same movement. That remarkable lay order, Opus Dei (of which more later), as well as Catholic Action, provide human material for a Christian Democratic movement. Sanchez Julia is all brains and will, for his body is terribly maimed by a circulatory disease that has led to successive amputations of his feet, legs and hands. This has been going on for twenty years.

There is little one can say about the leftist political movements in Spain over these few decades, for they have been so crushed and harried and are regarded with such hostility that they have the greatest difficulty in surviving at all. We must remember that a British Tory would be considered the most dangerous sort of radical by the Franco regime.

Liberalism is there, in its various forms, and it may well triumph in our day, but it can have no public, organized expression now. Franco (like the Communists) rightly sees it as his greatest danger.

Spanish socialism, which was always very mildly Marxist

like the British Fabian type or the French movement, is by no means dead. In fact, I was assured that the once powerful Socialist trade union confederation—the General Union of Workers (UGT)—still has clandestine strength in its traditional stronghold of Madrid.

Anarcho-syndicalism, whose center was in Barcelona, on the other hand appears just about dead. It looks as if the unique phenomenon of anarchism has run its course in Spain. It will always have some intellectual and emotional appeal, but it was too impractical even for the Spaniard.

And what about communism? After all, to believe Franco & Co. they fought and won a great victory against *los Rojos*—the Reds—and their slogan to this day is *"Comunismo, no! Franco, si!"* (Communism, no! Franco, yes!)

Of course, there is and always will be a Communist movement in Spain as in every country in the world. We have them at the South Pole this year. And, of course, they are to be feared everywhere, for behind them is the power of the Soviet Union and the ideology of Marxism. Having said this, it must be added that the Franco regime has been successful in keeping communism down to a minimum. It is in no sense a menace, nor could it become one even after Franco, barring the over-running of Western Europe by the Russians. Spanish communism merely has, and will have, a nuisance value to Moscow.

As is to be expected, there is a well trained cadre, or nucleus. The propaganda is skillful, and mainly comes through Radio Pyreneo Independiente, which apparently originates in Czechoslovakia. It signs off with the stirring "Hymn to Riego"—the Spanish "Marseillaise"—that one hates to see borrowed by totalitarian communism. This program is given twice a night and is in addition to the regular Moscow radio in Spanish which broadcasts Russian and other news two or three times a day. The broadcasts show the Reds to be well informed, with a knowledge of what is happening down to disputes in factories and their names. There are some clandestine publications, but they are printed in France and come in irregularly.

Spanish Reds who are sent in from outside never stay more than two or three months; by that time the police can be expected to get on to them. Then fresh ones come along. They work hard in the universities and have won a student following. After all, the students of today have known no other regime than Franco's and they are kept in ignorance of political movements. They have no means of knowing that fascism and communism are sisters under the skin and that the Communist professions of support for liberalism and a popular front are merely tactical. The stupidity of the anti-Communist campaigns waged by the regime and the Church (which controls education) makes communism attractive and interesting to the inquisitive, restless young mind.

The situation has been somewhat complicated by the growing relationship between Spain and the Soviet Union. Trade is increasing; delegations are exchanged; Spanish refugees who lived in Russia since the Civil War have been returning to Spain.

Most of all, there is the extraordinary and significant existence of hundreds of millions of dollars of Spanish gold lying in the bank vaults in Moscow. That gold presumably will go to any Spanish Government recognized by Moscow.

There has been a great deal of nonsense written about this treasure. The man who obviously knew most about it was Juan Negrín, the last Premier of Republican Spain, who made the dramatic gesture in his will of turning over the documents for the gold to General Franco.

The pre-war treasure of the Bank of Spain was officially reported in 1935 at $734,000,000. The amount that went to Moscow in October 1936 may have been as much as $600,000,-000, but was probably less. The Loyalists knew that they could not safely send the gold to New York, Paris or London after the Republican Government had to move from Madrid. Russia was the only friendly country which could be counted upon to keep the gold in safety and allow the Loyalists to draw upon it as needed.

So it was decided to ship the treasure—a great part of it in gold coins—to Moscow. Largo Caballero was still the Prime Minister and he insisted on signing the document for the deposit in the Gosbank of Moscow. Negrín, as Minister of Finance, felt he should have signed and kept the document, but Largo overruled him. One of the two signers for the Russians was, in fact, the Commissar for Finance. However, Largo claimed it was a matter for both the Foreign Minister and the Ministry of Finance and hence, by Spanish custom, to be handled by the Prime Minister.

Indalecio Prieto was, at that time, Minister of Marine. Negrín's idea was to send the gold in batches so that if any ships were captured or sunk, only a part would be lost. Prieto, however, insisted that it should all go in one convoy for which he guaranteed to provide a heavy naval escort.

Warships and freighters were then gathered at Cartagena, on the southeast coast where the gold had been sent from Madrid in September 1936, and Negrín and Prieto went to Cartagena to superintend the operation. The Rebels, seeing the concentration of ships, knew something was up, although they did not know what. Italian bombers were sent over from the Balearics that night to bomb the harbor.

As it happened, Prieto was always very frightened by bombs. He insisted that the group of them take refuge in the thick, old naval headquarters building. They groped their way to the very center in the dark—and discovered the next day that they had been standing in the patio under a glass roof!

At any rate, Prieto did provide a safe and heavy escort which took the ships through the Sicilian Straits to Tunis, after which there was no danger. The gold sailed on to Odessa and thence to Moscow.

Some of it was used to pay for the food, raw material and arms shipped by the Russians to the Loyalists. It is often forgotten that there never was any generosity on Stalin's part. The Russians charged for everything and asked such high prices that a number of the charges were still in dispute when the war ended. Moreover, a final shipment of arms, worth about $60,000,000, was, with many delays and with reluctance, allowed through France at the very end of the Civil War, but so late that none of it could be used and it was then shipped back to Russia. A credit was due for this.

In addition, Negrín discovered to his dismay after some months that the Russians were not only melting the coins into bars but charging an exorbitant mintage price for doing so. Since coins are worth more per weight than bars, he stopped that process, and protested the charge that the Russians were demanding, which was a considerable amount.

For these reasons no one—literally no one—can today name a figure for the gold in Moscow. It can only be reached by negotiation. Negrín would never even hazard a guess. My own would be between $350,000,000, and $500,000,000. When we consider that even after Franco Spain's gold and dollar reserves were multiplied in the last three or four years, with American help, the total is only $140,000,000, one can imagine what this amount means.

It is there in Moscow; it belongs to Spain and will return to Spain some day. Title to it was held by the shadow Government-in-Exile in Paris which did not touch it after the Civil War. There were only three sets of documents of the deposit, one held by the Russians, one by the Spanish Government and one in the Spanish Embassy in Moscow.

Negrín told me that he kept asking Largo Caballero for the Government's documents, but Largo always refused. When he was overthrown he cleared out his office and took all his papers with him, including the precious receipt for hundreds of millions of dollars. So Negrín did the next best thing, having become Premier in turn in May 1937, and ordered Spanish Ambassador Marcelino Pascua in Moscow to send the documents in the Spanish Embassy, which the Ambassador did reluctantly.

I asked Negrín the last time I saw him, in July, 1956, what he would have done if Russia and Franco Spain established diplomatic relations—which did not seem so far-fetched at one time. The former Premier said that in such a contingency he supposed he would have to turn the documents for the gold over to General Franco, since, after all, the gold belongs to Spain. He had no premonition of death at that time but the problem obviously weighed on his mind. It would seem that he did not trust any of the Republican leaders in exile to keep the precious documents, least of all Indalecio Prieto, who had twisted the facts in the gold issue and who was personally hostile to Negrín. A man like Juan Negrín would not allow his feelings toward Franco to outweigh his patriotism. So, he arranged that the receipt for the gold be turned over to the Caudillo. It was a very Spanish gesture and one that will be recognized as such, even though the Republican exiles were naturally dismayed by the action. In any event, the receipt by itself was not enough to permit Generalissimo Franco to collect the gold. The Caudillo is too committed to anti-communism to come to terms with Moscow, but it is extraordinary to think that Spain can, so to speak, become rich overnight by an accommodation of that sort. It shows the extent to which Spanish pride and the personal power of the Caudillo decide the fate of Spain.

The power is almost unlimited. This does not make Spain a totalitarian country in either the Communist or Fascist sense. It is an authoritarian country. The authority is exercised by keeping all parts of the regime weak or in conflict with each other. Order is kept essentially because the Spanish people want it, and through the Army and police. This makes Franco's power supreme when he wants to exercise it. Since, like all modern dictators, he does not allow any single man or group to become strong and threaten his power, there is no alternative to Francisco Franco, at least no visible alternative. As long as his position is not attacked and the nation's affairs function smoothly, he keeps hands off.

Moreover, it is not now a cruel regime, nor a police state in the Communist or Nazi sense. I know of several cases in which men, in the past year, were arrested, tortured, held without trial for months and still languish in prison or were released without explanation. However, although once common, this is now rare.

The prevailing tone in Spain for years has been apathy and tranquility, but everyone says what he pleases. It is this that gives a surprising atmosphere of freedom in a country that could hardly be less free in the fundamental civic rights—what Martín Artajo called the "secondary" liberties.

Freedom of the press is an example. Under a law of April 22, 1938, while the Civil War was still on, the state was given complete control of newspapers, magazines, books, motion pictures, manuscripts, radio and even musical scores. The one exception in all Spain is *Ecclesia*, the official organ of the Catholic episcopacy, which is exempted from censorship by virtue of the Concordat, but which applauds censorship of everything and everyone else.

The Spanish press is one of the greatest insults to the intelligence in the Western world. How could it be anything else under the stultifying pressure of both an obscurantist Church and a Government which uses the press as an instrument of politics and has a horror of free expression? There are plenty of first rate newspapermen in Spain. It is quite an experience to spend an evening with the editor of an important newspaper, to hear his informed, fresh, critical and sometimes brilliant comments on affairs of state and on the Caudillo, and then to read his dull sycophantic, bombastic newspaper the next morning. I had plenty of experience with exactly the same phenomenon in Fascist Italy, and then went back to see those same men turn out a lively, free press. I hope to do the same in Spain.

The rarest bird in Franco Spain is the sincere, dedicated believer who has nothing to gain from the regime but who is honestly convinced of its virtues. Many Spaniards consider a Franco-type dictatorship necessary in present circumstances, but this does not mean that they like it or are proud of it. They accept it; they either see no alternative or fear the possibilities that they do see.

This is the average Spaniard who has been passive and

apathetic for eighteen years. He is more often than not intellectually and emotionally anti-Franco. The forces opposed to the Franco regime embrace virtually all intellectuals, most university students, most (perhaps nearly all) workers, all the Monarchists (who are fed up and tired of waiting) and all the powerful regional forces of Spain—the Basques and Catalans above all, but also the Andalusians of southern Spain, who live in a feudal society of a very few rich and a great mass in dire poverty.

It is true enough that this deep, brooding discontent, the human being's instinctive reaction to misery, is an ancient grievance in Spain. Over the centuries visitors have always exclaimed at the dire poverty in Spain and the patient endurance and dignity with which it was borne. But this is the twentieth century; men have learned that dire poverty is a social evil due to the mismanagement and immorality of other men, and that it is not the will of God. This was one good lesson that the Second Republic taught Spanish workers and peasants. Franco has met this challenge, in part, by social services, the gift of a paternalistic state, but the fact remains that there is still an appalling degree of dire poverty in Spain to this day.

It is highly significant that younger elements in the clergy are championing the worker and peasant in this regard, and that outstanding members of the hierarchy also issue admonitions now and then. What is interesting is that the feelings of the young priests often lead them into a positive anti-Francoism, which is going to stand the Church in good stead when the day of reckoning comes.

And as I remarked before, large elements of the younger Army officers are also part of the opposition. Their day will come.

The basic force holding the Franco regime together is fear of another civil war or grave civic strife, although a new generation has grown up that did not know the Civil War. Spain illustrates what protean forms fascism can take. This is truly a unique situation—a military dictatorship strongly but voluntarily resting on the Church.

The fact that there is overwhelming opposition to the Caudillo does not mean that Spaniards want the outside world to settle their affairs for them. On the contrary, it was a colossal mistake for the democratic and Communist powers to try to overthrow Franco from abroad. Spaniards simply and naturally closed ranks. Moreover, they feel strongly about those who would sacrifice the well-being and even the lives of other Spaniards to stir up opposition to Generalissimo Franco.

The Spaniards of these postwar years have not been revolutionary. They could become so over night, but only through some inner compulsion. They will take care of their own affairs.

vi.

THE ECONOMY

GENERALISSIMO FRANCO SHARES WITH ALL MODERN dictators a complete ignorance of economics and finance. He saw what the demands of industrial workers and peasants for a better standard of living and a fairer share of the economy could do in a political and revolutionary sense. Consequently, he was not going to allow the workers to organize, to have free trade unions or to fight for their rights by collective bargaining and strikes. The worker, like the soldier, had to be well taken care of, but this was the duty and right of the paternal State, not of the free individual.

Being a very poor country and heavily damaged by the Civil War, Spain under any government would need a great deal of economic planning. A dictator like General Franco, who is trained to plan military campaigns, is naturally predisposed to other kinds of planning. The true Fascists like Mussolini and Hitler had a socialistic streak in them. Nazism was, indeed, "national socialism." The military dictators, like Franco and Juan Perón of Argentina, had no social philosophy; all they had was paternalism and—in Perón's case especially—demagoguery. It was the left wing of the Falange that espoused a philosophy of social progress in Spain, but that type of Falangist has been a critical and disappointed man for years. Franco leaves economic progress to others, except where the problems touch politics and public order or create a conflict between ministries that he must resolve. His interest lies, first, in the security of his regime and, secondly, in his concern for the welfare of the worker through the social services.

It is often said that one of the pillars of the Franco regime is formed of the big businessman and the big landowner. Certainly they support the Caudillo. As a group, and allowing for honorable exceptions, they are a rich, upper-class, corrupt and socially selfish element. In a sense, it is not their fault that they have been isolated from the contemporary trends in business and agriculture that are transforming economies which not so many years ago were as backward as Spain's— those of Italy and France, for instance. Spain, until recently, was barred from the Organization of European Economic Cooperation, the United Nations, the International Labor Organization and dozens of other economic organizations of international cooperation. This is being remedied now, but meanwhile Spain has had an economic structure that is just about the most backward and isolated in Western Europe.

Now, at last, it is changing and this is one of the most important developments in Spain today. The economy is being modernized and is improving slowly but steadily, and the United States deserves a major share of the credit. All signs point to a continued improvement over the coming years, although there is grave danger from inflation.

Spanish economy is passing through a belated transformation from the nineteenth to the twentieth century and is being hit by all the classic problems. She can never be a rich country, for the natural resources are not there, but the standard of living can be raised considerably and there can be a better distribution of wealth. There are signs that these developments are coming through the efforts of the Spanish people and largely in spite of the Franco regime. In addition, as remarked before, American aid is playing a big role. Spain went through six years of war and a five-year postwar period without any outside help. Not until 1951 did the Spanish economy start to grow at a good rhythm, and that was the year American help began.

Having said this, one must hasten to stress the slowness of the improvement, the dire poverty of most Spaniards, the dependence on the most unpredictable and the driest weather in Europe, the extremes of a few wealthy and the poor masses, the social selfishness, the corruption, the government restrictions on commerce, the grave inflation, the serious imbalance of foreign trade, the budget deficits, the discontent of labor, the antiquity of industrial equipment and the worst transportation system in Europe.

Each one of these factors could make a chapter by itself. Corruption is still rife in Government and industry. Some high officials have enriched themselves shamelessly. Everything is personal. One must know how to deal with the right person. Only too often, the law applies to the uninfluential, the weak and the poor, not to the rich. Spain has no well trained, permanent civil service like France, Britain and Germany. The civil servants in Spain are so badly paid that almost all must carry an extra job; many are corrupt.

Agriculture suffers from a lack of machinery, fertilizers, irrigation, erosion control and seed selection. Only 8 or 10 per cent of the arable land is irrigated. Industry is retarded because of low productivity resulting from lack of know-how, a high-cost structure, the absence of up-to-date machinery and equipment and the scarcity of foreign capital. The railway system is so antiquated that it cannot even satisfy the minimum demands of the economy. Some of the locomotives in use are a century old and their over-all age as a whole is very high.

It must seem strange, in view of these facts, to say that the Spanish economy is improving, but all things are relative, and an analysis of the Spanish situation today does show that it is getting better, especially in certain basic fields—agriculture, electric power and transportation.

The Franco regime presents the usual irony of the postwar era (it applies to the United States as well) of being a welfare state while professing horror of anything that smacks of socialism. Government planning covers more than half of the industrial structure through the operations of the *Instituto Nacional de Industria* (INI), founded in 1941. State-owned enterprises control a substantial percentage of the output in nearly every basic industry. Of the new capital raised annually by flotation of securities in Spain, the Government takes 55 to 70 per cent. This is a higher proportion than the most socially-minded northern European governments ever absorbed.

Spain has the most complete and most elaborate system of foreign trade and foreign exchange controls this side of the Iron Curtain—and incidentally, it is riddled with graft. The Government controls wages, hours, working conditions and many prices of essentials, although a number of price controls and all rations were lifted in 1952. Methods of bilateral—really barter—trade that were abandoned elsewhere seven or eight years ago are still common. Foreign investments are severely controlled and are not encouraged, even though Spain needs them desperately.

This does not, strictly speaking, add up to a planned

economy. There is simply a great deal of rather haphazard Government interference and control of the economy.

It is hard for Americans to realize the poverty of Spain. The annual per capita gross national production is $255, less than one-half the average of other European countries and about one-seventh of the United States. There has been a great deal of inconclusive argument about whether the average Spaniard is better or worse off today than he was before the Civil War in 1936. The United Nations Economic Commission for Europe estimated several years ago that the Spanish industrial and agricultural workers have a standard of living 10 to 30 per cent lower than before the Civil War, even with the social services. On the other hand, a First National City Bank report for July 1956 said that the real income of the average Spaniard is 25 per cent higher than it was before 1936. Foreign experts who have lived in Spain for decades, like the British author, Gerald Brenan, and the journalist, Henry Buckley, are convinced from their observations that Spaniards are better off now.

Statistics are unfortunately of no help. There is no statistical method of finding out where Spain is, what her national income amounts to, or where she is going. Each ministry will provide different statistics—if any.

The poverty of the average Spaniard is historic; it is classic; every traveller has remarked on it, with well-merited praise for the pride, dignity and patience with which misery is borne. There has always been hunger in Spain, and in some ways the economic system is constructed on the abstemiousness and the low standard of living of the people. I have heard it called "organized hunger," as if the economy could not carry on unless Spaniards went hungry.

At a certain level a low standard of living is not degrading or an evidence of misery. There are only about 100,000 privately owned automobiles in the whole of Spain, for instance. To have to go without a car or a television set is no hardship. It is not even serious that a bank manager in Spain can just about afford a motorcycle while any factory worker in the United States owns an automobile. Spaniards do not, in their present social and historic period, ask for luxuries.

They do ask for enough food, decent housing, good working conditions, some education—in short, for what elsewhere are considered the basic necessities of life. The tragedy of Spain is that vast numbers of Spaniards are not getting these necessities in adequate form; the hope of Spain lies in the fact that the numbers who so suffer are steadily lessening and the future holds promise for better days.

Meanwhile, life is hard. The basic wage of an industrial worker or peasant ranges between the equivalent of 50 cents and $1 a day; social services would all add 25 to 50 cents. It is encouraging and honorable that some of the most earnest protests against this pathetically low remuneration have come from Spanish Church leaders and from priests in the Basque country.

In July 1953, Archbishop Marcelino Olaechea Loizaga of Valencia issued a detailed study of conditions in his province, to which he added sharp criticisms of employers who were encouraging communism by their selfishness. "We wish to point out," the Archbishop said, "that a worker and his wife (getting the maximum standard wage) can never hope to drink wine, afford any kind of amusement or spend money in car fare to and from work."

"Deprived of all but the necessaries of life, that worker's

existence can hardly be called human," he continued, "unless we wish his condition to be but slightly different from that of slaves."

The agricultural laborers in the olive groves and vineyards around Seville, I discovered last year, earn 25 to 30 pesetas a day (63 to 75 cents), and they have large families. Most of the land, in huge holdings, is owned by aristocratic and often absentee landowners, who are very wealthy. Melons are one of the products of the region and were plentiful at the time I was there. Even in the local market places they cost 8 to 10 pesetas apiece, and hence were a luxury beyond the reach of the peasants who grew them. Such things explain why Spain has had so much revolutionary civil strife in the past—and will have more in the future. It also helps to explain anti-clericalism for, despite the honorable exceptions, the clergy is with the landowner.

The distribution of wealth in Spain is so unjust that (to cite a few of the many figures) 83 per cent of the Spanish people account for less than one-third of the national income; the very rich, who are estimated at 5 per cent of the working population, account for 38 per cent of the national income; in Madrid, which is considered a high wage area, 75 per cent of the population is in the low-income bracket.

The Government has decreed sporadic wage increases, but each time prices rose and overtook the increases, leaving the worker worse off than before. That is what happened to the astonishing addition of 40 to 50 per cent to the total wage bill throughout industry, decreed last November 14th. On that basis, unskilled workers get 31 to 36 pesetas a day (78 to 90 cents), an average increase of about 25 cents. Since this is costing the industrial structure as a whole something like $450,000,000 extra annually, the answer had to be more inflation.

The inflationary trend has been going on for years. The rounds of wage increases, higher public and private investment, a step-up in currency circulation of 10 per cent a year since World War II, and regularly unbalanced budgets all contribute to inflation. Budget deficits are financed by bond issues to private banks, which cause an inflationary base. Government-owned industries pay the wage increases with new currency.

It has been a parlor game in the last three or four years to blame the United States for the inflation. This was easy to do, for we have poured money into Spain at a great rate since 1951, and particularly since September 1953 when Spain became our military ally.

The impact in any given locality of United States aid is, of course, inflationary. It is this that mainly gives the impression that the United States program contributes to rises in wages and prices and to shortages of labor. However, there is a distinction between a few local situations and the economy of Spain as a whole. In the latter respect, the aid program is deflationary and there is reason to complain that the Spanish people have not been told the facts. Government officials are frank to concede the value of American aid in private conversations, but they do not advertise it.

Spain had a run-down economy when United States Government aid began with a $62,500,000 Export-Import Bank credit, authorized by the Mutual Security legislation for 1951. Defense Support Assistance totaled $230,000,000 through the 1956 fiscal year, and another $50,000,000 was allotted for the 1957 fiscal year. The sale of United States agricultural sur-

111

pluses in Spain amounted to more than $100,000,000 each year in 1955 and 1956—cotton, edible oils, tobacco, corn, potatoes, lard and other necessities, to be paid for in pesetas.

It is hard to see what Spain would have done without this aid. It saved the country from great distress and from severe inflation.

United States money brought in large quantities of consumer goods and far more resources than the Americans used up, in fact, an estimated total of four times as much. Only 6 per cent of the materials used in the bases program is being bought in Spain. The United States even brings in its own cement and the food the Americans eat. Fewer than 10,000 Spanish workers in all are being used in the program, which hardly makes a dent in Spain's labor force. United States aid is helping to tide the country over the effects of the disastrous freeze of February 1956, which destroyed more than half the citrus crop.

Spain's climate is a curse. Droughts, freezes and the unpredictability with which these plagues strike are sore trials. The effects of droughts can be controlled up to a point by irrigation, reservoirs and the digging of wells, and this at last is being done on a large scale. It will be a long time, however, before Spain is free of the hazards of droughts. Between 1940 and 1953, for instance, there were seven seasons of extreme drought. Since 75 per cent of the electric energy is supplied by hydroelectric plants which are dependent on rains, each time there is a drought industry suffers heavily.

There was a catastrophic freeze in February, 1953, and then the one last year which was estimated to cost a loss in exports of citrus fruits and olives amounting to some $80,000,000. Since Spain has a trade deficit, and citrus fruits account for 15 to 20 per cent of the total, a setback of that sort is calamitous.

Moreover, such freezes damage the trees for a few years, which means that this year's crops of fruits and olives are necessarily poor. There has not been a really good olive crop since 1951. Spain has had to import much cottonseed and soya bean oil to mix with olive oil for home consumption. With the best of luck, it will be 1958 before the position is recovered.

To be sure, the Franco regime must bear a due share of the responsibility for the poverty of Spain's agriculture. Gross mishandling at the Government level in the early years, the worst black market in Europe, a failure to push programs for mechanization, irrigation, housing, reafforestation and fertilizers until recently, a failure to tackle the ages-old social and economic grievances of the peasants—all these factors explain in part why Spanish agriculture is so backward and deficient.

Spain is not poor in land—only 11 per cent is unproductive—but in the centuries of neglect of that land and its inefficient cultivation, and in the outrageous treatment of its peasants. As was pointed out before, the Spaniards never had the sort of revolution that led to the great landed estates being broken up and those who till the land owning it. In England, France, Mexico and many other countries there have been such revolutions or evolutions. In Southern Italy a sensible, democratic Government is putting through such reforms peacefully. In Spain the Second Republic started to do it in a crude, bungling way, and after the Civil War began, in areas controlled by the Loyalists, there was much seizure of land by peasants. But, of course, Franco turned that clock back immediately, and the peasants involved were lucky if they survived.

Spain is now seeing many agrarian reforms in a technical sense—irrigation and resettlement, reafforestation and watershed control, land consolidation and improved methods—but

113

the peasant is still a secondary citizen and is yet to derive the same benefits from the social services as the industrial worker. Nearly half the people of Spain earn their living from the land and yet agriculture accounts for less than 30 per cent of national income. Only since 1951 (the year American help began) has agricultural production exceeded the 1930-1935 norm, and even then it did not keep pace with the increase in population from 25,000,000 to 30,000,000.

In studying simple and basic problems like this one grasps how the Franco regime has held Spain back and what a price the country is paying for "law and order." The wheat acreage, for instance (wheat is Spain's leading crop) equals France's, but the yield is less than one-half. Animals do nearly all the drafting work in Spain, for only one in 200 farms have tractors. Grain is sown, cut and threshed by hand on all but a few farms.

Holdings in the North are too small to be economic (minifundia) and in the South there are enormous estates (latifundia) owned in a great many cases by absentee landlords. Only 28 per cent of all Spanish farmers work their own land. Nearly one-half are casual laborers. The percentage of workers on the land is one-third more than the European average and two-thirds more than that of the United States—which gives an idea of the inefficiency of Spanish agriculture. It is estimated that there are about 1,000,000 surplus workers on the land for whom work must be found in industry; otherwise their standards will continue to be pitifully low. It is hard to see any reason in this day and age why Spain should be so far behind the rest of Europe in technical know-how.

Yet, one must keep on stressing the fact that the situation is improving and has been improving since 1951, the year in which United States aid began. The 1953 military agreement calls for an investment of at least $400,000,000, even if the program is not expanded, as it may well be.

At this point we are only considering economic aid, which has been concentrated on the three great bottlenecks of agriculture, electric power and transportation, and on the sale of surplus American farm products under Public Law 480. When "Defense Support Aid"—really economic aid grants—are voted, Spain only gets 30 per cent of the amount in dollars. Sixty per cent goes to the Americans for base construction and 10 per cent to administrative expenses in the form of counterpart funds, which is to say pesetas that are spent in Spain.

I do not see how anyone, studying the position for Spain as a whole, can claim that American aid is inflationary when its over-all effect is so clearly deflationary. Spain needs that aid desperately and prices—especially food prices—would certainly be higher without the American imports.

Generalissimo Franco's greatest headache in the field of labor, however, comes not from the agrarian but from the industrial side. This is natural in an era when workers in all countries have become aware of their rights and of the benefits of a free trade union system. Spain has nothing remotely approaching labor freedom. All workers are organized under the Falange syndical system whose rules have been drawn up by Franco and whose leaders are all Government appointees. The laborer often gets justice and a fair deal, and he has an excellent system of social services—but he is not free, and what he gets is the gift of the Caudillo, not his acknowledged rights.

It must be conceded that the labor troubles of recent years have been essentially economic, not political. That is to say, the workers have not risen for revolutionary reasons, to overthrow Franco, but for higher pay, better conditions and protection against the inflation which outpaced their rises in wages.

At the same time it is obvious that when it is illegal to strike—as it is in Spain—a worker risks his freedom as well as his job, and now and then his life, to protest. In this sense, strikes have a political connotation, and a very serious one for General Franco.

The strikes in the Basque country in April 1956, for instance, and earlier strikes in Barcelona in the Spring of 1951, were clear danger signs to the Franco regime and were recognized as such. Spaniards are the last people in the world to drive to desperation; they would blow Franco and his regime sky-high overnight and the Caudillo knows it.

In the Basque country last year it was interesting to see the parish priests (not the hierarchy) support the workers. In fact about fifty Basque priests signed a letter to Pablo Gurpide Beope, Bishop of Bilbao, asking permission to support publicly in their sermons workers' demands for higher wages. The Bishop denied their request. A great many priests were transferred from their parishes afterward.

In their letter, the priests pointed out that "the difference between the purchasing powers of the present salary and what should be the minimum earning power of the workers is appallingly unjust. For the last twenty years [i.e. the Franco regime] Spain's workers have reaped nothing but disillusion."

Yet the Basque workers are the best paid in Spain. The heavy industries, like iron and steel are concentrated there. Catalonia is the great textile center of Spain and is also highly industrialized. That is why, when one hears of labor troubles, they are almost always in Catalonia or the Basque country. However, Madrid has become more and more industrialized since the end of the World War. A lack of fuel and adequate transportation would seem to rule Madrid out as the "New

York of Spain," but it is certainly impressive to see the amount of building taking place in the capital.

Madrid workers are traditionally Socialist and doubtless will be again when they get the chance. The Catalans were Anarcho-Syndicalist, but are not going to revert to that outworn philosophy.

The Basques are the most progressive of all the workers and if there is anything that Francisco Franco hates to see it is progress in that sense. "Every Basque is a nobleman," as the saying goes. The caste differences, which are so notable in other parts of Spain, are almost non-existent in the Basque country.

What do exist are great differences in wealth—and the Basque is less resigned to take this than any Spaniard. The perennial unrest among the Basques is fanned by reports of high profits and public announcements of very favorable industrial developments. Workers read of an increase in the national income and yet they see a growing disparity between their wages and the price level. They have to work eleven hours a day to maintain a bearable standard of life while their employer gets wealthy.

In other words, the Basque worker, who is only in the vanguard in this respect, is demanding a fair share of the products and the profits of his work. It is an important development because it is part of the changing pattern of Spanish life. The Caudillo cannot stop it, which is why, instead of the announced 6½ per cent basic wage increase last autumn, he felt impelled to give one of 40 to 50 per cent.

And, as always, the organized workers are in a better position to get benefits than tradesmen, civil servants, intellectuals. I inquired about some salaries when I was in Barcelona. An assistant professor at the University got the equivalent of $43 a month last year; the Dean of the Faculty of Letters and Sciences got $144 a month; the best paid newspapermen received $72 a month. Is it any wonder that intellectuals, civil servants and all classes of Government employees must have two or three jobs?

It is only fair to point out that all salaries and wages are greatly helped by the social services. This is the best feature of the Spanish labor situation. To be sure an American, or a European from France, Britain or Scandinavia, cannot help getting a slight pain in hearing Spaniards boast about their social services. The democracies have done so much better than the Fascist and Communist countries that there is no comparison. Any regime in Spain would have done much in this line; it is part of our twentieth-century philosophy of labor.

Such being said, it must be conceded that substantial progress has been made in housing, public health, social insurance, cooperatives and education. Social security covers such items as accidents, health and old age insurance, family allowances, cost of living bonuses, marriage grants and paid vacations. It is good enough to meet International Labor Organization standards.

The enormity of the problems has to be recognized, to be fair. Spain is, after all, a very poor country. Dwelling units for workers have been built at an impressive rate, and yet housing is still a major social problem in Spain and the program is not even keeping pace with the normal population growth. Employers with payrolls of over fifty persons are now requested by law to house 20 per cent of their employees.

One always must return in Spain to the truism that all things are relative. That is why one can say that, despite all these drawbacks, the Spanish economy is improving—and this is a very important thing to be able to say. The Cabinet was reshuffled on February 26, 1957, mainly to install Ministers who would cut Government expenditures and put a brake on inflation.

The situation is better and on the way up in the iron and steel industry, electric power, transportation (railway and highway networks) and agriculture. Spain will remain vulnerable to the effects of drought for years, but this vulnerability is gradually being lessened, and more and more efforts are being made to industrialize. Spanish industry was 90 per cent dependent on hydroelectric power not so many years ago; now it is down to 60 per cent. The freezes are unavoidable, but citrus growers are switching to cotton.

Consumer standards have risen a little; tourism a great deal. Between 1950 and 1955 the number of tourists rose from 750,000 to 2,500,000. Americans will be surprised to know that they rank fourth, with less than 250,000 although to be sure they spent well over $30,000,000 in 1956.

Industrial production expanded nearly 11 per cent in the 1950-1955 period. The general trend of exports is upward, despite last year's freeze, but the foreign trade position is chronically weak. The per capita value—about $37 per inhabitant in 1955, for example—is the smallest in Western Europe. The trouble is that Spain's major exports are luxury agricultural products (like citrus fruits, olives and olive oil) and raw materials for which world demand is variable and dependent on prosperity.

Spain's credit position is good. Thanks to American aid, her gold and dollar reserves trebled to a total of $225,000,-000, but had declined to $140,000,000 last winter. For many years there was a flight of capital, but it decreased and now there is, on balance, a considerable repatriation.

Economic isolation, like political and military, is ending. Spain is now a member of the United Nations and she is gradually becoming a part of O.E.E.C.

No one can say that Generalissimo Franco has solved Spain's principle economic problems, but they are gradually being solved without him. It is a sort of "Operation Bootstrap," like Puerto Rico's. An inner strength is slowly developing. Change is coming, if gradually. Ancient methods of agriculture are slowly being improved. Industrialization is making steady progress.

Moreover, the United States is now committed to a long and extensive program of aid.

vii.

THE AMERICANS

"ONCE UPON A TIME THERE WERE THREE BIG, BAD fascists—Mussolini, Hitler and Franco. We fought a World War to kill two of them and to destroy all they stood for; now we have made an ally of the third."

A future historian, with a flair for the ironical, could write just that and still keep close enough to the facts. Even those who for practical, military reasons championed the American agreement with Franco Spain for air and naval bases, would have to concede that this is the irony of fate. For those who always did believe in General Franco, who supported his cause in the Civil War, who excused or explained away or even praised his relative neutrality in the Second World War, and who have seen him as the Christian paladin, leading the anti-Communist crusade, the shift of American policy was right and natural. For the rest of us—the majority in the United States and Western Europe—it was a shock or the regretful acceptance of what seemed like a military necessity.

On *The New York Times* we opposed the treaty as long as there was any chance of preventing it but once the agreement was made there was nothing for it but to accept the situation and hope for the best.

The arguments against making the pact ceased to have practical value. Once a decision was made to subordinate political and moral considerations to military, the die was cast. The Pentagon said it needed air and naval bases in Spain; Government policy had to conform to this necessity—for the security of the United States is a primary necessity. From that moment the policy and attitude of the United States toward Franco Spain had to change.

If one considers the non-Catholic, 80 per cent of the American population, the sentiment toward Generalissimo Franco and his regime has at all times been hostile. Even the Roman Catholic 20 per cent is by no means united in admiration for the Caudillo. President Harry S. Truman, like Franklin D. Roosevelt before him, shared the common American antipathy toward Franco and made no bones about it—although he, too, yielded to reasons of state when the time came. Mr. Truman tells us in his memoirs, when describing a discussion on Spain at the Potsdam Conference, that "I made it clear that I had no love for Franco." Winston Churchill, as well as Joseph Stalin, expressed similar sentiments. President Truman repeated them on occasions, even in 1952, his last year in office, but this did not prevent him from accepting the negotiation of the military pact or, previously, from sanctioning the return of an American Ambassador to Madrid. Our envoy, like others, had been withdrawn in conformity with a United Nations resolution in December 1946.

In November 1950, after the futility of this silly measure had been well demonstrated, the General Assembly revoked it. Early that year, Secretary of State Dean Acheson, whose personal sentiments were always anti-Franco, explained with his customary brilliance and good sense why the United States would go along with this action.

"The United States," he wrote in a letter to Chairman Tom Connolly of the Senate Foreign Relations Committee on January 19, 1950, "has long questioned the wisdom and efficacy of the actions recommended in the 1946 resolution. . . . In retrospect it is now clear that this action has not only failed in its intended purpose but has served to strengthen the position of the present regime. . . . Our vote would in no sense signify approval of the regime in Spain."

Republican Senator Arthur H. Vandenberg, in a statement supporting Secretary Acheson's course, said much the same thing: "It is not a question of approving the Franco regime. We have never done that and we do not now."

Mr. Acheson made a significant proviso: "At the same time," he wrote, "it is difficult to envisage Spain as a full member of the free Western community without substantial advances in such directions as increased civil liberties and as religious freedom and the freedom to exercise the elementary rights of organized labor."

Alas! the best intentions of the best statesmen "gang aft agley." It never made any sense to say these things, and we shall see how far the reality departed from these pious hopes.

On July 16, 1951, the late Admiral Forrest Sherman, U.S. Chief of Naval Operations, went to see the Caudillo in Madrid. His visit had been approved by the President, the Secretaries of State and Defense, the National Security Council and the Joint Chiefs of Staff.

There was such a hullabaloo, in Europe as well as the United States, that Mr. Acheson felt it necessary, two days later, to explain that "Spain is of strategic importance to the general defense of Western Europe," and it had been thought wise to undertake "tentative and exploratory conversations." He conceded that the United States had been unable to agree on the matter with France and Britain.

Very soon military and economic missions were on the way. On August 30, we made one final and futile effort to oppose the policy in a long editorial in *The Times*.

"Having fought the greatest war in history to defeat fascism are we now in such desperate straits that we must take a fascist regime as an ally?" the editorial asked . . . "There is no use fooling ourselves with the belief that the United States Government can go on insulting the Franco regime with hard truths about American opinions of fascism. We would have officially to abandon our critical attitude. One of the clear facts that Americans must face is that if we go ahead with this arrangement, we will be helping to perpetuate Franco in power as long as he lives and cares to remain the Dictator of Spain. This will be our responsibility in the face of history."

The contemporary world has judged us in exactly that light. Actually, after my last visit to Spain, I convinced myself that American aid did not save Generalissimo Franco personally, nor is it prolonging his tenure today. The more I thought about it the more obvious it seemed to me that if the Generalissimo could survive the trying years of the Second World War and the even more trying six postwar years of economic misery and political ostracism, he could survive anything. Spain needed our help and we saved the country from great distress and a much worse inflation than she has had, but the elements that could have come along to throw out Francisco Franco simply were not there. Furthermore, he has certainly shown himself eminently capable of handling opponents.

We did build up Franco and his regime; we did rehabilitate Franco Spain and play the decisive role in making it a respectable member of the community of nations. With our military pact, the Caudillo became an ally of the greatest democracy in the world; with our backing, Spain became a member of the United Nations and a number of affiliated organizations. Franco Spain is no longer a pariah among the nations of the world, and for this United States support and the policy behind it are largely responsible.

One irony of the situation is that General Franco always said that he knew he was right and that he would not change in any way to satisfy the requests and hopes of the democracies. Thereupon we proved that he was right; because without changing his policies one iota, we went to him, dealt on equal terms and gave him a most advantageous military and economic pact without the Caudillo making any political concessions whatever. As I remarked before, the mountain went to Mohammed.

Even at the time the military agreement was signed, in September 1953, the intention was to keep Spanish-American relations cool and correct. The pact and its annexes were made precise in every detail. There was, in theory, none of the warmth shown to old allies. Anything more, it was said, would not be an expression of the feelings of the American people. After the agreement was signed it had to be made clear to Spaniards that it did not in any way weaken our links to our traditional allies or NATO. This statement was suppressed in the Spanish press.

The American officers and diplomatic officials then and now have stressed the fact that the 1953 agreement was strategic—and, of course, it was. The strategic value of Spain to the defense of Western Europe is obviously considerable. Any tyro looking at a map can see that. The air bases put us within 3,000 miles of the industrial heart of the Soviet Union.

The naval base at Rota, seven miles north of Cadiz on the Atlantic coast, will for the first time establish the United States as a Mediterranean naval power. It will be the only United States Naval base in Europe where carrier-based planes can be landed and serviced. The Sixth Fleet will now have a home of its own in Europe where warships can be refitted or have major repairs.

The bases run in a diagonal line about 500 miles long, northeast from Rota. Three of them are large Strategic Air Command bomber bases for the United States Sixteenth Air Force—one twenty-five miles southeast of Seville at Morón de la Frontera, one at Torrejón de Ardoz, fifteen miles northeast of Madrid, and one at Sanjurjo-Valenzuela a few miles north of Saragossa in Aragon. In addition there is an airforce supply base at San Pablo, seven miles outside of Seville. An oil pipeline, 485 miles long connects all these bases from a huge "tank farm" at Rota to the air base at Saragossa.

On the margin of this basic program will be minor but important features such as ammunition and supply dumps for the Navy at Cartagena on the east coast and at El Ferrol and La Corunna on the Bay of Biscay in the northwest. There will be an "early warning" radar and aircraft control network on the Island of Majorca and at points on the peninsula, and a microwave communications system. Finally, the Americans are helping the Spanish Air Force to improve its own airfields.

The headquarters, under Major General August W. Kissner of the U.S. Air Force, who directed the program from its inception, are at Madrid.

This is a formidable undertaking, and will not be completed in 1957, although Admiral Sherman started the ball rolling back in July 1951. The negotiations took more than two years. Aside from normal complications, the Caudillo was a tough bargainer and he wanted to have his Concordat with the Vatican out of the way before he signed and sealed the military pact. The Roman Catholic hierarchy of Spain, especially the fiery and fanatical Archbishop of Seville, Pedro Cardinal Segura, were opposed to the agreement. It meant that thousands of American Protestants would come into Catholic Spain and this was dreaded. The Concordat was signed on August 28, 1953; the Spanish-American military agreement on September 26, 1953.

It was the high spot of Francisco Franco's career. So far as he and most Spaniards were concerned, he had won. He had defeated his enemies in and out of Spain; he had refused to yield one inch of ground to the forces of the liberalism he so despised, and now his efforts had gained the highest sanction from the two highest powers in the world, religious and secular —the Vatican and the United States.

Six more months of planning, hard bargaining and frustration were to pass before the American program really got under way. The original schedules for construction were ridiculously optimistic and had to be drastically revised. It had been hoped that the bases would be finished long before this. Two winters of abnormally wet weather provided the worst setbacks of all. Construction virtually ceased.

In May of 1956 the fine dry weather set in and all along the line work went ahead at a steady pace. By the time I made the rounds in August it could safely be said, for the first time, that the constructors were over the hump. The weather could no longer stop them in any serious way. The pipeline has now been laid all the way and the builders are "out of the ground" at the bases.

By the summer of 1957 the United States will have a network that could function in part in an emergency. By June,

1958 the program should be finished in all vital respects. That will make nearly five years since the signing of the agreement, which only runs for ten years. However, there is a provision to extend the pact automatically for two successive periods of five years each unless one side or the other wants to cancel it, which can be done with six months consultation and a year's notice.

The naval base at Rota is the most ambitious and costly part of the United States program in Spain. Of the $400,000,000 allotted for the bases as a whole, the one naval base is costing $120,000,000.

Rota has been facetiously and unfairly called "the American answer to Gibraltar," which is just a short distance around the cape. The reference to Gibraltar makes Spaniards shudder, for if there is one thing that they made clear to the United States negotiators from the beginning it was that "we will never let this become another Gibraltar."

No United States flag has been allowed to fly over this or any other base in Spain. As is the case at every United States base, the nominal commander at Rota is a Spanish officer. This was provided for in Article 3 of the pact which said: "The areas which by virtue of this agreement, are prepared for joint utilization will remain under Spanish flag and command." The American officers supervise "United States personnel, facilities and equipment." Since the "facilities and equipment" are, in reality, the bases, this does give the American commanders the authority they need. But they must exercise it with due care for Spanish pride.

Secretary of the Air Force Harold E. Talbott discovered this to his chagrin on two occasions. He said on a visit to Madrid in November 1953, when asked by a newspaperman, that the United States would stock its Spanish bases with atomic bombs. The Spanish press immediately let out such a howl that the Secretary felt impelled to disavow his statement. This was apparently more than the Spaniards thought they had bargained for. Yet, the runaways I saw being built—and I saw all of them—will be capable of handling large jet bombers.

The other *faux pas* Mr. Talbott made took place in Washington the following January when he was asked by a reporter whether the agreement with Spain did not provide only for the peacetime uses of the bases.

"Well, who's going to stop us?" Talbott replied. "There are certain agreements on the use of the bases, but when the balloon goes up we are going to use them."

Since the Spanish-American agreement clearly stated that "the time and manner of wartime utilization of said areas and facilities will be mutually agreed upon," the Secretary had to explain later that the United States would, of course, live up to the terms of the agreement. In other words, the wartime use of the bases depends on the consent of Generalissimo Franco or whatever Government succeeds him.

As a matter of fact, Americans and Spaniards are getting along wonderfully well. The first command of all the missions is: "Maintain and foster Spanish-American relations." Spain has often been a European battleground, but always an inhospitable billet to foreign soldiers since the Phoenicians and Greeks subdued the Iberians. In fact, Spaniards do not like their own troops either. They are allergic to uniforms, and with good reason. Their armies in modern times were ingloriously led abroad and used against the people at home. The idea of 10,000 to 12,000 American military men in Spain—which will be the final figure—is something to worry about.

Meanwhile, the American officers take care to go around in civilian clothes and wear their uniforms as little as possible.

They have orders to be friendly, but no orders are necessary in that regard with Spaniards, who dislike foreigners in general, but who are as courteous, open-hearted and hospitable to strangers in particular as any people on earth.

Some of the Americans are naturally going to have it better and easier than others. Saragossa is a typical Spanish provincial town as removed from any experience that North Americans have had as any place that could be found in Europe. The Iberians, the Romans, the Visigoths and the Moors, all in their turn, spent centuries there and left their imprints. Out of the mixture came the Aragonese—dour, reserved, hardy and "provincial" in a literal sense. They were slow to take the Americans to their hearts, for they are the type of people who make friends slowly, but they were won over in time. In a social sense it is going to be a hard post for the Americans and their families who are going to live there, as there is little to do. The air is dry, dusty and fierce with the heat in summer, but in winter it is bitter cold with the piercing *cierzo* (north wind) that prevails in those parts.

Seville is quite a contrast. The city itself is one of the show places of Europe, with its lovely mixture of Arabic and Spanish architecture, its ancient Jewish quarter, its innumerable nooks and corners that enchant the strolling visitor. The Andalusians are as different from the Aragonese as the Neapolitans from the Piedmontese. They are a warm, friendly, voluble race speaking a Spanish which is a bit different than the Castilian that all the American officers must learn. One sees in Seville where the Latin American pronunciation of Spanish comes from.

History goes a full circle in this area. Columbus used Seville as his supply base for his voyages to the New World, and now we are using it. Columbus's ships sailed from ports very close to our new base at Rota. One has a sense, in that part of Spain of the history that links the New World to the Old.

The Americans come in fresh and eager to please, which is fine so far as the Spanish people are concerned, but rather disconcerting on the political side. Having been ordered peremptorily to keep out of politics—a necessary order, of course—the American officer or civilian arrives with no more idea of what has happened in Spain or what kind of a Government the Franco regime is than a new-born babe. His early contacts are with high officers or officials, and in Madrid, at the headquarters, they rarely become anything else. Most Americans in Spain are too young to have been aware of the Civil War while it was happening. The version they all hear is the Government one—"Franco saved Spain from the Reds, etc." The interpretation of politics is along the line that Spain needs a strong hand at the helm, she is not ripe for democracy, the Franco regime is benevolent, everybody loves Americans and is happy to have the military agreement.

Even the religious side of affairs is clothed in a certain rosy distortion. The anti-Protestantism is not felt because of the friendliness that the Americans meet whatever they are. In any event, by a natural, and perhaps partly calculated, system of selection Spain gets a far higher proportion of American Roman Catholics than is to be found in the American armed forces as a whole. It is desirable to have men who speak Spanish. Besides, officers or non-coms who have Spanish-speaking wives—Latin American, Filipino, Spanish—are urged by the women to seek assignment to Spain, and since they, too, usually know the language, they are favored. Such men would almost always be Catholic.

This is a wise policy on the part of the United States, as

a matter of fact, and it is helping to get the program off to a good start. However, it will not be possible to keep it up later when 10,000 to 12,000 American military men have to be sent to Spain and rotated.

As Americans make friends with ordinary Spaniards in posts like Saragossa, Seville and the towns around Rota, they get a slant on politics that is more realistic than their first naïve beliefs. Whether they bring up the subject of politics or not, their Spanish friends would certainly do so. Some Americans, like those at the early-warning posts and naval supply bases like Corunna and Cartagena, are really going to be isolated, as Americans, and they will hear what Spaniards truly feel and believe. The Spaniard is the reverse of sly or hypocritical; he always says what he thinks and feels.

Spaniards are by no means unanimous in agreeing that this alliance between our two countries (which is what it amounts to) is wholly good for Spain. Everyone agrees it is good for the Pentagon and for the regime of Generalissimo Francisco Franco, but it means an end to Spanish neutrality after 150 years and a dependence on the United States that frightens many persons. They point out that they were able to remain neutral in both World Wars and they do not see why they cannot continue to do so if there is another World War. They naturally do not relish the idea of atomic and hydrogen bombs being dropped on Spain because they have an alliance with the American "Colossus of the North." The Franco regime is completely committed to being anti-Communist and anti-Russian, but future regimes may not feel so strongly about it. Moreover, as I said before, Spaniards do not like foreign troops on their soil, though they are there by voluntary agreement and are not occupying troops. Nor do they like the thought, however unrealistic, of one or more "American Gibraltars," even temporary ones.

In a minor sense, one ought to add a certain amount of resentment and envy at seeing all these "rich" Americans, with their cars, their money to burn, their standards of living so far above the average Spaniard's. This is a problem the Americans have to face everywhere abroad, even in England, but it has to be taken into account at all times. At least, it can truly be said that in addition to the military program we are doing our best to help Spain economically and to raise her standard of living.

Whatever Spaniards feel about the military pact, no one I ever met in Spain thinks that a United States policy aimed at making Spaniards hungry and unemployed would weaken General Franco. It may be over-subtle to say so, but it can certainly be argued that the stronger the Spanish people get the weaker the Caudillo's position will become. A man who must devote all his thought and energy to getting enough to eat for himself and his family is not going to be a threat to the Generalissimo. The well-fed man thinks about politics and has the energy to do something about it. And when a Spaniard thinks about politics he is anti-Franco, with rare exceptions.

However, the value of the United States aid should not be underestimated. As the figures given in the previous chapter show, we are spending at least $400,000,000 for the military bases, have supplied $230,000,000 in economic aid since 1953, with another $50,000,000 coming this 1957 fiscal year, and have provided something like $225,000,000 surplus farm commodities to be sold against pesetas.

There is, at least, unanimous praise for the economic aid, although the Madrid Government has expressed it privately rather than publicly. This program made things easier for General Franco, although, as I said before, he has amply demonstrated that he can remain Caudillo the hard way.

What are we Americans getting out of it all? On the strategic side the American military leaders are unanimous in feeling that they have made a splendid deal. This is especially so since Morocco became independent. On maps and charts and in theory, the Pentagon is certainly right, but if I was an American general I would cross my fingers and say to myself: "Beware of Nemesis!"

The bases, it will be recalled, can only be used in time of war by mutual—which is to say, Spanish—consent. Hitler and Mussolini thought they had a close understanding with the Generalissimo but when "the balloon went up" in World War II, they were left on the ground. We can feel very happy that this was the case, but it does not provide a comforting precedent for the future.

Francisco Franco is a most cautious, a most coldly calculating man. If or when the time came, he would do nothing impulsive; he does not make gestures. He will weigh the various factors involved and decide whether it is good or bad to go along with us.

We must remember that the agreement was made with him and him alone. He is the Government of Spain. No one can possibly say what is coming after General Franco. There is hardly likely to be stability for some time. The future Government may feel like the Moroccans who now say that we made our pact to build the Moroccan air bases with the French, not with them—and that was true.

In other words, we are taking a calculated risk. I am not arguing that this was avoidable or that the risk should not have been taken, if the Pentagon is right in saying that we must have bases in Spain.

It is ironical now to think of Dean Acheson's letter to Senator Connally in 1950. More than seven years have passed and Spain has not taken a single step "in such directions as increased civil liberties and as religious freedom and the freedom to exercise the elementary rights of organized labor."

Are we doing anything about it? On the contrary, we see such things as Secretary of State John Foster Dulles going out of his way unnecessarily to visit the Caudillo in Madrid on November 1, 1955, and then issuing a communique about "frankest cordiality and reciprocal understanding," "American friendship for Spain," "the spirit of collaboration."

We do not try to rehabilitate Hitler or Mussolini; we do Franco. We are not cool and correct with him; we are cordial and flattering. This was always what had to happen. We were saying the obvious on *The Times* when we wrote that "we would have officially to abandon our critical attitude."

As I saw when I went from base to base and at headquarters in Madrid, all criticism was abandoned privately as well as officially. Most Americans were won over to the idea that Franco and his regime were good for Spain.

Naturally, we were never in a position to say to the Caudillo: "We despise you and everything you stand for, but we would like to build some naval and air bases in Spain." That was never realistic. In aiding Marshal Tito of Yugoslavia we could be utterly matter of fact. Our attitude toward communism was crystal clear. We had no illusions about it or about him, and he frankly proclaimed his intention to remain a Communist. The arrangement was enormously valuable to both of us and it was always kept on a purely practical basis.

We have not contaminated each other, so to speak, and there never was any danger of doing so.

That is the way it naturally would be with communism. But what about fascism? Obviously, we take a different attitude. We not only have a number of allies in Latin America who are fascists or the equivalent, but we would never lift a finger to prevent a Latin American country from going fascist. When little, weak Guatamala threatened to go Communist, we moved in and staged a revolution against the Government.

There are some of us who consider fascism as bad as communism. In America there is much more danger of fascism than communism.

Generalissimo Francisco Franco is (to use a good new word) fascistoid, with an unsavory political record and an evil reputation throughout the democratic world, and it is just too bad that we have to join up with him. Anyone who walks with the Devil must watch his step very carefully. Granting that we had to make this deal we ought, in our minds at least, to be as clear and frank about it as with Marshal Tito. We have made a bargain with one of the most tenacious and outstanding enemies of democracy in the world—in order to defend democracy.

In this century and in these times the lure of totalitarianism is strong. We Americans are safe from it today, but in a war or in a serious economic crisis, the danger would become great. We must keep in mind that fascism and communism are the Janus-faces of one body. Hitler saw that as long ago as the early 1920's when he was writing *Mein Kampf*.

"In our movement the two extremes come together," he wrote, "the Communists from the Left and the officers and students [Nazis] from the Right." In August, 1939, he proved his thesis by making an alliance with Stalin.

The enemy is totalitarianism, not just communism. The struggle for liberty in the world cannot be won until both communism and fascism are defeated. Since we have had to make an arrangement with General Franco we should never forget that. As we are going to sup with the Devil, let us be sure to take a long spoon.

viii.

THE CHURCH

"SANCHO," SAID DON QUIXOTE TO HIS FAITHFUL COMPANion, "we have come up against the Church!"

Every Spaniard has done so before and since Cervantes wrote that immortal line. One could no more think, or talk, or write about Spain in the past 1,200 years and ignore the Church than one could ignore the Spanish people. From the time the Moors invaded Spain, the Church has played a great role in Spanish history. And it was a great institution in its time. Most of the New World was Christianized by Spanish priests, and Latin America remains Roman Catholic to this day. The Catholic faith of Spain was not shaken by the Reformation and it was Spain that led the Counter Reformation.

Somewhere a process of fossilization set in. The Spanish Church became, in a sense, a national Church, linked to the Holy See but different in its fierce orthodoxy and its refusal to move and grow with the times. Catholicism has survived for 2,000 years partly because the Vatican has known how to accept and adapt itself to the change and progress taking place in the world. Accommodation, tolerance, flexibility, patience, diplomacy—the Holy See could always call upon these characteristics when necessary. Not so the Spanish Church which has been a reflection of the extremism of the Spanish character.

The so-called "Black Legend" that runs through history and commentaries since the sixteenth century is a result of that extremism. Only Spain could have had the Inquisition in such a drastic form; it is in Spain today that Protestants are treated as damned souls; it is in Spain that anti-clericalism takes the form of church-burnings and the killing of priests and nuns as it has done on various occasions in the last 130 years.

At the turn of the century there was a Right-wing political party, called the *Integristas,* led by Ramón Noceval. Its members said a rosary every evening for the "conversion" of Pope Leo XIII whom these fanatics considered a Socialist because of his famous encyclical, "Rerum Novarum," which put forward the progressive social ideas of modern Catholicism. Surely, it is only in Spain that such a thing could happen.

When the Second Republic was created in 1931, the Papal Nuncio, Mgr. Federico Tedeschini (now Cardinal), reached a *modus vivendi* with the Government. For this he is still reviled in clerical and monarchist circles. Yet his action seemed to show that the Vatican was in those days perfectly willing to accept a relationship between Church and State which approximated that of all other Catholic countries. It was Spain that changed herself with Generalissimo Franco's victory in the Civil War, and the Vatican went along.

Under the Monarchy, the few Protestants in Spain were able to print and circulate their Bibles freely. In 1940, the Franco regime confiscated all the Protestant Bibles they could lay hands on. The British and Foreign Bible Society in Madrid managed to bring in some Bibles for their followers after the World War. On April 24, 1956, the authorities seized these, and all efforts made by the British Embassy to get them back have failed. It was claimed that some of the books had contravened Spanish printing regulations, but these were imported books. The real reason, as Foreign Minister Martín Artajo told me, was that there were more than necessary for distribution to Protestants and hence they seemed destined for proselytism.

The well known Jesuit Father Cavalli, in a definitive article on "The Position of Protestants in Spain," published in 1949, made the point that, "When freely annotated and interpreted, and presented as the sole basis of Divine Revelation, the Bible becomes the main instrument in the Protestant campaign and onslaught against the Catholic Church." At any rate, Spain is surely the only country in the world where the Protestant Bible is banned, because of Protestantism.

There is, of course, no freedom of worship in Franco Spain. Politics, even more than religion, made this a necessity. The Spanish Church always supported feudalism, monarchism, centralism, authoritarianism, the aristocracy, wealth. The hierarchy today devolves from the Counter Reformation, when the Catholic Church in Spain was saved by its close alliance to the throne and by a rigid censorship that kept the peasantry ignorant as well as poor. Through its grip on education (only temporarily interrupted by the Second Republic), the Church has sought to inculcate qualities of obedience, acceptance of the established order, suspicion of modernity. The dynamism of this vital, individualistic people has been damned with the help of the Church, which has at most times in its history concerned itself too much with material possessions. Until the last century it was a great landowner. Now its wealth lies in businesses, real estate, newspapers and the generous Government subsidies it gets under the terms of the new Concordat.

That Concordat was a great triumph for the Caudillo, and it was interesting to see how belatedly he got it. After all, he was the "Paladin of Christianity," the great crusader, and he had restored the wealth and privileges of the Catholic Church even before he had conquered all of Spain. It seemed as if the Vatican wanted to be sure that General Franco was here to stay. The Holy See was always uneasy and critical of Spain's ultraorthodoxy. However, it is at all times neutral toward politics. Its concern is with freedom for the Catholic Church, not with freedom per se. Whether a government is democratic or dictatorial is unimportant. What matters is its attitude toward religion.

Under the Spanish Republic, Church and State were separated and religious liberty was decreed. The Vatican accommodated itself to this, but the Spanish hierarchy fought the measures step by step as the Constitution was being formulated. Then came the anti-clerical outbursts of the Popular Front and the Civil War, with many priests and nuns killed and many churches burned.

Naturally, the hierarchy and clergy were fiercely pro-Franco. After the Loyalists established order such excesses stopped. Priests and nuns could not wear their robes but they were allowed to say mass and even tend their flocks without molestation in most parts of Republican Spain. The Loyalist Government even tried hard to get the Vatican to accept an open agreement on freedom of worship, but there was too much bitterness by that time. I met nothing but incredibility in writing these things at the time, even though I saw them with my own eyes and knew them to be true.

One typical and very Spanish item did not come to my knowledge until long after the Civil War, but I was able to verify it on my last trip to Madrid in August 1956. I am sure it will seem incredible to my readers, yet it is true.

One of the most famous of the Communists on the Loyalist side was La Pasionaria—Dolores Ibarruri—the Basque widow of a worker, whose natural eloquence, courage and fervent Marxism made her one of the most colorful and important of the Red leaders on the Republican side. Afterward she fled to Russia, where she has lived ever since. Her son was killed in the Second World War fighting in the Russian Army.

In the early, desperate days in Madrid, when priests and nuns were being killed, La Pasionaria spirited a number of nuns off to a house in Alcalá de Henares. She also arranged to establish an apartment house in Madrid as an extra-territorial building under a foreign flag and placed many nuns in it. In both cases the sisters were cared for in safety and then allowed out of Spain along with other refugees.

That was *muy español*—very Spanish. All human nature is complicated, but I sometimes think that the Spanish character is the most complicated of all.

It took two and a half years of secret negotiations before the Vatican and General Franco came to terms. Then the Concordat was presented to the Spanish people on a take it or leave it basis—and many Spaniards did not like it. They thought it gave the Holy See too much. The previous Concordat of 1851 had, at least, been adopted after free and full discussion in the press, on the public platform, and in the Cortes, but that is not the way Generalissimo Franco works.

He felt very satisfied because it gave him great prestige and the last, reluctant support of the deeply Catholic people who had thought that something must be wrong if the Vatican refused to make a Concordat with Franco. He not only got his Concordat but was awarded the Supreme Order of Christ, the highest Pontifical decoration. The pact was signed on August 28, 1953, and I have already noted its connection with the American military agreement.

This is no place for an analysis of the Concordat, but there are three features that need to be noted at this point because they are dominant and affect the contemporary situation.

The Concordat is essentially an economic document so far as much of its content is concerned. The Church receives an annual subsidy as indemnification "for past alienation of ecclesiastical possessions and as a contribution to the work of the Church in favor of the nation." All Church land, buildings, treasures, printing presses and the like are exempt from taxation. These provisions are protected so as to be guaranteed regardless of the economic status of the country at any given time.

The iron-clad grip of the Church on education is reinforced in the Concordat. Spain is unique in this feature of her life, which takes one back to the Middle Ages. Spanish education is certainly the most backward and inadequate in Western Europe. Teaching "must conform to the principal dogmas." "The Spanish State guarantees the teaching of the Catholic religion, obligatorily, in all institutes of instruction, whatever their rank or grade and whether they be State or non-State schools." The Church authorities will supervise all schools to be sure that "the purity of the Faith, good morals and religious education" are maintained. The teachers, the books, the curricula for this education are under the direction, which is to say, also, the censorship of the clergy.

Thirdly (and actually this comes first in the Concordat):

"The Catholic, Apostolic, Roman Religion continues to be the sole religion of the Spanish nation and it will enjoy the rights and prerogatives due to it in conformity with Divine and Canonical Law."

These features lead into three remarkable aspects of Spanish life—anti-clericalism, the status of education and anti-Protestantism.

The question of the wealth of the Church has for centuries been a sore point with Spaniards. One must recognize that the clergy needs considerable revenue to run churches, monasteries, schools and other institutions. The popular belief that the Church has wealth in excess of these needs and that it fattens on the country's revenues while the people lead harsh and hungry lives has contributed to the extraordinary force of Spanish anti-clericalism.

Generally speaking, the anti-clericalism of Spain has not been anti-religious. The Anarcho-Syndicalists and the Communists of modern times are about the only exceptions to this rule. The Spanish Socialists were theoretical Marxists and hence theoretical atheists, but not real ones.

Anti-clericalism in Spain far antedates the birth of Karl Marx. Its true basis is in the social and economic spheres; it is primarily a class reaction. A Spanish worker or peasant will say: "The Church is rich; we are in misery. The Church supports the oppression of the Government [whether it was a King or, as now, a Caudillo]; therefore we are against the clergy. But we are Catholics and remain Catholics."

Generation after generation this mentality has been formed and whenever in modern times the bayonets that guarded the Monarchy and Church were removed, there was a terrible popular outburst. Church burnings and the killing of priests and nuns, in their modern phase, go back to 1835, a century before the latest Civil War.

There is, too, an intellectual anti-clericalism—liberalism, in short—which first took pronounced form with the "Generation of '98." This calls for a separation of Church and State, an end to the Church's monopoly on education, the curtailment of the wealth of the Church, and the removal of the many special legal and economic privileges of the Church. This is what took place under the Second Republic and it explains a good deal of the hostility of the Spanish Church and the Vatican to the Republicans.

Now, the identification of the Church with the Franco regime is complete; hence to be anti-Franco sometimes leads automatically into anti-clericalism. It sometimes, but much more rarely, leads to conversion to Protestantism. Religion is so bound up with the State and the Church is so powerful that it takes daring in small communities and parishes, where one is well known, to stay away from Church on Sundays and holydays, especially if one is middle- or upper-class.

The extraordinary power of the Church today is a source of anxiety to many thoughtful clerics. I have already mentioned the weekly called *Ecclesia* in Spain, which is the organ of the Spanish episcopacy and of Catholic Action. It is literally the only publication in Spain free of censorship. This has sometimes led to remarkably frank and pungent attacks on the Franco regime and sometimes to the exercise of the magazine's power to make sure that no other publication is allowed the same privilege of a free press.

Anti-clericalism, therefore, has no outlet—no press, no free speech, no teaching of free thinking in the schools. The Spanish hierarchy—at least some members of it like the enlightened Bishop of Malaga, Angel Herrera, an ex-editor and newspaperman—have argued in favor of some freedom of the press as a means of letting off steam.

Ecclesia has been worried by something more subtle. Again and again in recent years it has referred to what it calls "religious inflation," by which it means that perhaps the Spanish Church has been given a position, a power and a wealth beyond what is good or right for it, beyond the modest treasures of material goods and humble faith that the country possesses.

I have not been, in my own United States or in Britain, France and Italy, where I have lived for many years, remotely anti-clerical. We have no reason whatever to be so in countries where there is separation of Church and State, freedom of worship, free education and where the economic status of the churches are commensurate with their needs and their roles in society. It is not the perversity of the Spanish character that causes such profound anti-clericalism in Spain. Spaniards are instinctively a deeply religious people.

A student of Spain can only be amazed and heartsick at seeing generation after generation of the Spanish clergy repeating the same mistakes and building up the same forces of hatred that take such a terrible toll when the lid blows off. As of today, it is Generalissimo Franco who sits on that lid, and I met few Spaniards who denied that when he dies there is going to be another explosion of anti-clericalism.

However, I did find a widespread belief that this time the reaction will not remotely approach the ferocity of 1936. I am convinced of that myself. In fact, if General Franco can hang on long enough, there may be little or nothing to fear.

The reasons for this are partly to be found in the people and partly in the clergy. In some subtle way, and for reasons hard to pin down, the lay Spaniard is less fanatical today than he was twenty or twenty-five years ago. Years of enforced quiet, a broadened outlook on life, a greater sense of responsibility, a better understanding of social forces—whatever it may be—there seems to be less propensity to violence than when I first went to Spain. This may be a surface appearance; only time will decide, but meanwhile some elements in the Spanish Church are working to correct the medieval attitude of a large part of the hierarchy.

One of the truly significant things happening in Spain today is that the Church is changing, not in its faith, not even remotely in a movement of protest against Rome, but on the contrary, in a movement toward Rome.

I have remarked before and it is, indeed, one of the clichés of religious history that the Vatican has for four or five centuries been trying to restrain the excesses of Spanish orthodoxy. In modern times it has tried to bring the Spanish hierarchy to accept the social and economic advances that have been commonplace in all Catholic countries, at least since Pope Leo XIII, seventy-five years ago.

Today the Spanish Church is at last moving from the fifteenth to the twentieth century. One sees it primarily in the younger priests, whose education has given them economics, politics and a vision of the modern world. The older priests, some now bishops, archbishops and cardinals, were trained in another predominantly theological world and in a social system that found the Spanish Church allied to the upper classes against the people, or at least divorced from the people.

In their sermons today many priests are preaching an advanced social and economic philosophy. Priests who organize football games and even charity bullfights were unknown ten or twenty years ago but they are now becoming common. The gap between the clergy and the people is narrowing.

During the strikes in the Basque country in the spring of 1956 many Basque priests came out for the workers. Although their Bishop stopped the priests sternly and recently transferred 200 Basque priests from their parishes, the workers are not likely to forget the events of last spring.

This sort of thing was necessary, for during the reprisals and trials after the Civil War the clergy in too many instances showed little or no Christian mercy and did not attempt to temper the severity of the Nationalist reaction. This is remembered by the workers and Loyalists. Even in the case of the Basque strikes, many workers are more likely to remember the harsh, uncharitable attitude of their Bishop rather than the sympathy of their parish priests. Moreover many Basques do not forget that General Franco had twenty Basque priests executed during or after the Civil War for sympathizing with the Loyalists.

Yet it is only fair to note that the Church has always promoted social welfare and has fairly consistently fought a battle for higher wages and better standards of life. *Ecclesia* has led the way in its sharp criticisms of conditions.

After an investigation a few years ago it found that an "overwhelming majority" of Spanish workers were not practicing Catholics, that "the Marxist virus rusts his soul," that he leads "a bitter life, especially about material things" and that he prefers "to see the priest aloof from politics." It even conceded that those workers who understood such problems preferred a separation of Church and State. The Archbishop of Valencia, Mgr. Marcelino Olaechea Loizaga, recently estimated that "three-quarters of the workers have no religion whatever."

The Church, in short, still has a long way to go before it wins the active benevolence of the Spanish workers and peasants. However, this is still true in countries like Italy and France where the citizen has nothing to fear from the Church. In all these Latin countries, and above all in Spain, the women are the main source of the Church's popular strength. Spanish society, as I pointed out, is based on the family.

Another common phenomenon in all these countries is the anti-clericalism of the intellectual. This is understandably most pronounced in Spain, for the most obvious reasons. A Spaniard to whom culture, thought and education mean anything is naturally outraged by the combination he is up against in Franco Spain today—an educational system virtually monopolized by an obscurantist, almost medieval Church, with the backing of a Government that does not permit freedom of press or speech.

The censorship would be incredible in any country but Spain. Everybody censors everything—the Church, the Government and the Army. How could Spain have anything but the worst press in Europe, a daily insult to the Spanish intelligence? How could Franco Spain permit any writers or artists of stature to grow? Artists can only work in freedom. The same thing has happened in Russia, in Nazi Germany, Fascist Italy, Peronist Argentina. It will always happen. At least these other countries had no ecclesiastical censorship.

When a first rate novelist like José María Gironella produces a trilogy on the Spanish Civil War, he is only permitted to publish the first volume, *The Cypresses Believe in God,* because it merely deals with the period before the Civil War. The two volumes on the Civil War have been banned. There are some good poets working in Spain today, but working in fields which are not "heretical" or "subversive," or at least too popularly political.

The best artists and writers lived out of the country or spent years outside, and they have been hostile to Franco. José Ortega y Gasset and Pio Baroja, Picasso, Luis Quintanilla, Pablo Casals, Juan Ramón Jiménez (who won the last Nobel Prize), Rafael Alberti, Ramón Sender, Salvador de Madariaga.

It is the Jesuit Order that has the strongest grip on education, above all in the elementary and middle schools. Their grip on the universities has been loosened in recent years by the rivalry of other orders and above all by the workings of a remarkable lay order known as Opus Dei.

Opus Dei (its formal name is *Sociedad Sacerdotal de la Santa Cruz et Opus Dei*—Priestly Order of the Holy Cross) was founded in Spain in 1928 by a wealthy and high born priest, José María Escrivá de Balaguer, who is now in Rome and head of a world-wide organization. There are branches in the United States at New York, Chicago, Boston and Washington. The American head is Father Múzquiz, Spanish born but now an American citizen.

In 1947, Opus Dei received the approbation—the *decretum laudis*—of Pope Pius XII, and in 1950 there was a Vatican decree granting it definite, official approval. The order claims it is the first secular institute elevated to the category of a pontifical law and the first to get such approval.

Because it is semi-secret the Falangists, who do not like it, dubbed Opus Dei the "White Freemasons." It is not really secret, but it does not publish any statistics about its numbers or its resources. Its members do not advertise their membership, although they do not hide it if asked.

The members are an intellectual and social élite who are becoming powerful in academic circles. The unmarried members who form its basic cadre, must vow poverty, chastity and obedience. The vow of chasity brings the normal popular suspicions that Opus Dei attracts perverts. Married persons cannot become full-fledged members. They are affiliated— *agregado*—and cannot become a part of the central and ruling organizational structure.

Opus Dei is rich. The founder was wealthy and the order receives much from its members who are supposed to give whatever surplus they have above their simple, bachelor's or spinster's life. There is a common fund for these contributions.

The women's section is totally parallel and independent of the men's, except that both are headed by the President-General of Opus Dei in Rome, now Mgr. Escrivá. In the individual countries a Consiliario (a priest) is in charge. Both in Rome and elsewhere a majority of the staffs are laymen. Member priests wear no distinctive robe or sign.

There is no reason to believe that Opus Dei is very influential in Government circles; no Cabinet Minister or very high official is a member so far as is known. However, there is a widespread belief in Spain that Opus Dei is a power behind the throne.

The members of the order live a somewhat religious life like the tertiary orders of the Franciscans and Dominicans. Their activities are of two kinds: first, religious, such as special retreats; and second, educational. Opus Dei has a university in Pamplona. It is also training the clergy to get a better, more cultured type. It encourages "late vocations" of doctors, engineers, lawyers, and such. Members follow their trades and professions freely and they do not deal with politics except in that they are anti-Communist. After General Franco, Opus Dei is expected to get behind a Christian Democratic movement; in the meanwhile the order keeps out of politics.

It is an important organization to keep in mind because the signs point to it playing an interesting role in the future of Spain. After all, it is a true élite, made up of professional and educated people, not the masses. It already has great influence in the universities where it is trying to snag as many chairs as possible. Opus Dei sees to it that bright young members have assured futures in the teaching profession.

Its natural enemies are Catholic Action, the Falangists and the Jesuits. In these cases Opus Dei is cutting into territory where there was no previous challenge. It is doing much to raise educational standards and also to raise the intellectual level of the clergy and to broaden the outlook. These are worthy aims.

As a Church movement goes, Opus Dei has some claims to being liberal. It tries to abolish class distinctions and it is not a bigoted order. Where bigotry makes its most striking display to an outsider is in the attitude toward Protestantism, and especially toward the Spanish Protestants. In a population of nearly 30,000,000, the Government estimates there is a total of only 25,000 Protestants. Of these probably 9,000 are foreigners. Yet Protestantism is treated as if it is a great threat to the Catholic faith of Spain.

Curiously enough, those of us who spent years in Spain during the Civil War never noted any antipathy toward Protestants or Protestantism. To be sure, the Republican Government had established freedom of religion and separated Church and State. All the same, if anti-Protestantism were a deep-seated, instinctive aversion or fear we would have felt it.

As a matter of fact, in 1937, at the height of the Civil War, Generalissimo Franco was advised to make a declaration that there would be freedom of worship after the war. He did, in fact, send a letter to the Duke of Alba, then his envoy in England, which was published in *The Times* of London. It said that if and when the war was won freedom would be granted to all denominations. Nothing came of the promise, of course.

On the contrary, in fact, as soon as the conflict ended in 1939, General Franco abrogated the Republic's Law of Religious Confessions and Congregations. Protestant schools were closed, although they had been permitted under the Monarchy. An accord that the Caudillo made with the Holy See re-affirmed four articles of the Concordat of 1851, declaring that Roman Catholicism was the sole religion of the country.

At that time, no rights were recognized for other religions. In 1945, the *Fuero de las Españoles* (Bill of Rights) was passed and it contained the nearest approximation to tolerance, one that has been the basis for endless discussion. Article 6 read: "None shall be molested for his religious beliefs or for private practice of his worship."

The key word here is "private." There never was any question of public manifestations or ceremonies—no Cross outside, no signs, no billboards, no listing, no advertisements and, above all, no proselytism.

Little as this gave the Protestants, it was bitterly fought by the fanatical Archbishop of Seville, Cardinal Segura. In fact, the Cardinal went so far as to say flatly in a pastoral letter in 1952 that Article 6 did not bind the conscience of Spaniards and would not, unless or until it was embodied in the Concordat then being negotiated.

It was. A final protocol to the Concordat stated that: "In national territory, the measure set forth in Article 6 of the *Fuero de los Españoles* remains in vigor."

This was one of the most striking manifestations by which the Vatican showed that it did not approve of the Spanish clerical extremism of Cardinal Segura and those who felt the way he did. The Archbishop of Seville is a fine, upright, well meaning and utterly sincere man, and I discovered on my trip to Seville last year how much he is loved and respected in his archdiocese. Nevertheless, he is a very narrow and bigoted man, living in a long-gone age, and most Spaniards are critical of him in that respect.

The fact that he has consistently been anti-Franco is held to his credit, but not his reasons for being so. Anyone who considers the Caudillo too lenient with Protestants or too modern in his tolerance of "wicked" institutions like dancing and the movies is very much out of step, even in Spain.

Cardinal Segura's fanaticism led to his being removed as Primate of Spain. The present Primate is Enrique Cardinal Pla y Deniel, Archbishop of Toledo, who is ardently pro-Franco and always has been.

The Caudillo softened the blow at the time the Concordat was ratified on October 27, 1953, by making it clear that his tolerance of Protestantism was limited. He said non-Catholics would be allowed to practice their religion only as long as their activities did not conflict with the "Catholic unity" of Spain.

"But," he continued, "this tolerance toward other creeds does not mean freedom of propaganda likely to foster religious discrepancies and perturb the safe and unanimous possession of religious truth in this country."

The accent, therefore, is on unity and against proselytism. Foreign Minister Martín Artajo, an intensely religious man, who was head of Catholic Action and who can be accounted as the leading Catholic layman of Spain, had emphasized the same points a month before.

"The majority of Spaniards," he wrote, "believe that

Protestant propaganda in Spain is an attempt of foreign pene-
tration in national life, directed with political aims at the
destruction of the religious [i.e. Catholic] unity that sub-
stantially exists in Spain and that is recognized by all
Spaniards."

He told me the same thing when I saw him in San Sebastián last year. Protestantism is a divisive force, he argued,
which is dangerous in a country with such regionalism and
differences of race as Spain. Catholicism is a great source of
Spanish unity. Moreover, as he rightly pointed out, Protestantism has a political connotation; it is one way of "protesting"
against the Franco regime. He also made the common accusa-
tion that the Protestants take a negative, destructive and of-
fensive attitude. "They always attack the Pope, the Vatican,
the Catholic Church, instead of merely expressing their own
religion."

There is a real drama behind the personal case of Señor
Martín Artajo, just as there was in the case of Secretary of
State John Foster Dulles. This extraordinary coincidence
throws light on the different attitudes of Spaniards and Americans toward religion.

Señor Artajo sent his son to Edinburgh University a few
years ago. Some months later the son wrote to his father that
he had lost his faith and, according to all the Spanish accounts
I heard of it, intended to become a Protestant. When the
Foreign Minister received this letter in his office in Madrid, he
fainted dead away and had to be revived by his associates.
That was how the news became public.

It was a truly dreadful blow to Señor Artajo, who had had
his whole family, like himself, educated by the Jesuits. Apparently a girl was involved. At any rate, so far as is known,
the son did not become a Protestant, but from the religious

point of view loss of faith is even worse to a deeply religious person like Señor Artajo. (In passing, let us take note of the cleavage that this incident typifies between the university students of today and their parents.)

Secretary Dulles' case was, so to speak, the reverse. He is one of the outstanding laymen in the Protestant faith of the United States, a leader in his own Presbyterian Church and in the National Council of Churches of Christ. The blow that struck him came when his son, Avery, became converted to the Roman Catholic Church, studied for the priesthood and was ordained in the Jesuit order last year. Mr. Dulles' first reaction, a natural one, was to break with his son. Later he made up and actually was photographed with the new young priest at the time of his ordination.

This could not possibly have happened in Spain. It is almost commonplace in the United States for families to have one or more members of different faith, Protestant and Catholic together. In Spain it is virtually unheard of, with very rare exceptions and then with a sense of shame and tragedy.

There is a classic joke that Spaniards tell on themselves and which anyone going around hears in a variety of versions.

It is about a girl who runs away from her home and widowed mother because she can no longer stand the misery and drudgery. A few days later her distraught mother gets a post card from Barcelona, saying: "Don't worry, Mother, I am all right and I will be coming home soon." Weeks later she shows up at the house. "Where have you been, you bad girl?," her mother scolds, "What have you been doing?" "I've been in Barcelona," the daughter answers, "and I became a prostitute [*prostituta*]." The mother goes positively frantic, bursts into tears and moans but, finally, she looks a little puzzled. "Daughter," she says, "tell me again. What did you become?" "A prostitute!" "Oh!" says the mother in a tone of great relief, "I thought you said Protestant [*protestante*]."

In Spain, a devout and cultured Spanish woman said to me: "A Spaniard is a Catholic or he is nothing." He can become an agnostic or even an atheist, but his mentality does not let him understand a "deviation" like Protestantism.

The result is that in spite of all the fuss that is made and despite reports to the contrary, there have not been many conversions to Protestantism in Spain. When they do occur they create sensations, like the case of Padre Carillo de Albornoz, a member of an aristocratic family. In the early 1950's he was head of the Jesuit Youth Associations in Madrid. He was then given a Papal appointment in Rome as head of all the youth associations in the world. Suddenly he went off to Switzerland and proclaimed himself a Protestant—it is believed a Calvinist—and got married. The effect on the young people in Spain is said to have been devastating.

However, the very sensationalism of that case is an indication of how unusual it is for a Spaniard to turn Protestant. Many Spanish Catholics do, indeed, ask why their Church is so afraid? It is literally in the strongest position of any "national" Catholic Church in the world. Its priests are far better trained than the few Protestant pastors, or even than the foreign Protestant ministers, some of whom come in as if they were missionaries. This infuriates Spaniards more than anything.

The bitter Church and Government diatribes against Protestants are, above all, aimed at the foreign missions and the financial aid that comes from abroad. When I was in Madrid last August, Jesuit circles were passing around, almost clandestinely for it was not given to the press or general public, a pamphlet called: "*Protestantismo en España*," 52 pages

illustrated, and a rather costly job. It did not have the im-
primatur of the episcopacy, but it was obtainable from Jesuit
headquarters opposite the American Embassy. Actually, it is
a poor job and most of the offending publications it cites
were printed and distributed in the United States and Latin
America, not Spain.

However, it was typical in its censure of foreigners who
give their money to Protestants in Spain. Yet Spanish Protestants could not exist without such funds. They have no legal
status and hence cannot own Church property. A Protestant
pastor could own a building or a house for use as a chapel,
but if or when he dies the property is personal and lost to his
flock.

A well known foreign Roman Catholic, who has lived in
Spain for thirty or thirty-five years, said to me: "I have never
met a rich Protestant Spaniard."

They cannot have their own schools. The Elementary
Education Act of July 17, 1945, permits non-Catholic schools
for foreigners only. During the Monarchy this was not the
case.

There was a Protestant Union Theological Seminary in
Madrid that before the Civil War had as many as 600 foreign
and mostly Spanish students, and was considered by some
intellectuals to be the best school in Spain. It was tolerated
for a while when it opened up again in 1947, but was so
harassed and boycotted that it was down to eight seminarists.
Yet even this was too much for the Franco regime. On January
23, 1956, the seminary was closed by order of the Ministry of
the Interior, and it has remained closed despite petitions from
several foreign governments, including the United States. The
Executive Committee of the World Council of Churches has

repeatedly protested in vain. Since no Protestant schools are legal in Spain, there is no legal basis for a protest.

It is hard for Americans to understand the Spanish attitude toward Protestants, even when one knows Spain well. To us, it makes no sense.

To them, Spaniards who turn Protestant are *"malas españoles"*—bad Spaniards. For one thing, they receive money from abroad. For another, they are looked upon as queer people. The average Spaniard outside the big cities has no contacts with Protestants and no understanding. Often the Spanish Protestants are ostracized. In reality, there is a great ignorance in religious matters in Spain. In the villages the peasants never in their lives meet a Protestant, and I am assured many do not even realize that Protestants are Christians.

While I was in Madrid last year an incident happened which showed that the anti-Protestant propaganda was getting down to the people. I am convinced that the average educated middle- and upper-class Spaniard could not care less, so far as his social contacts with foreigners are concerned.

A New Zealand priest was in Madrid on a visit, going around dressed, as American priests are, in trousers, coat and collar, and not in the long soutane, or cassock, invariably worn by Spanish priests. The New Zealander went up to an old woman vendor of cigarettes in the Puerta del Sol, whose poverty can be imagined, and asked for a package of cigarettes. "I don't sell cigarettes to Protestants," she said angrily. He was certainly angry himself when he walked away, but foreign Catholics are continually being dismayed by some of the manifestations of Spanish Catholicism.

It is almost amusing to hear someone in Spain say earnestly: "But some of my best friends are Protestants!" As with those who say in America: "Some of my best friends are Jews," one must suspect that the person is basically hostile. The Concordat refers to *"no-catolicos"* (non-Catholics). Spaniards almost always say *"disidentes"* rather than *"protestantes."*

The official attitude can perhaps best be understood in the ceremonies of marriage and burial. During the Second Republic only civil marriage was valid although it could, of course, be followed by a religious ceremony. Today, marriages performed in Protestant chapels in accord with Protestant rites are not recognized by the Spanish State, but the "full civil effect," to quote the Concordat, of marriages performed according to Catholic canon law is obligatorily accepted. Protestants must have a civil ceremony, having first proved that *both* parties are non-Catholics. Moreover, if one or both of the parties were born Catholic and converted to Protestantism there would still have to be a Catholic form of marriage, since the Church continues to regard as her subjects any persons who ever belonged to her.

Aside from the difficulties of worship, it is the attitude toward burial that most disturbs Protestants in Spain, for they are denied their rights even in death. There are only two types of cemeteries in Spain; the Catholic cemeteries are, of course, in consecrated ground. In addition, there is a "civil cemetery" where non-Catholics, Mohammedans, Jews, agnostics, atheists, suicides and unrepentant criminals are buried. In a large city like Madrid, such cemeteries are well kept. Pio Baroja, the novelist, who died last October was buried in the Cementerio del Oeste in Madrid, having been an agnostic and bitter anti-clerical all his life.

There have also been for generations four "extra-territorial" British cemeteries in La Corunna, Malaga, Bilbao

and Madrid. These, however, are so full now that there would
be no room for Spanish Protestants.

The civil cemeteries in small localities are usually a
railed-off plot in a corner of the Catholic cemetery. There are
many stories of the way they are neglected. Sometimes Protestants have to buy themselves a plot in a field and use it as a
burial place, but in that case the parish priest must turn a
blind eye out of compassion. A leading Protestant clergyman in
Madrid told a friend of mine that in some small provincial
towns there is only a common grave for non-Catholics. The
Information Service of the Federal Council of Churches of
Christ in America wrote some years ago that when there are
no civil cemeteries, "Protestants often have to bury their dead
in the fields," but I was assured that this is not so. The real
facts are bad enough.

Spanish Protestants need a great deal of faith and courage.
The hierarchy of the Roman Catholic Church in Spain perse-
cutes them for religious reasons; the Government for political
reasons. The only way they can fight for their faith is by
petition, for they have no means of defending themselves
within the law and as soon as they go outside they are
prosecuted.

They sent a long petition to General Franco on behalf of
"*el pueblo evangelico español*" on June 8, 1956, which was
being hotly discussed while I was in Spain last summer. It
covered all their grievances, which was a good reason for it
being a long petition. It kept stressing Article 6 of the Bill
of Rights, which is the one and only door to what little tolerance they receive. Unfortunately, this article is not precise
and hence open to arbitrary local interpretation. The same is
true with proselytizing; the petition asked that it be defined

so that Protestants could know what is permitted and what forbidden.

The conclusion contains sixteen requests. Here are some of them boiled down:

2.) Give us the juridical personality necessary to exist.

5.) Recognize the legality of Protestant marriages.

6.) In education, allow Spanish Protestants to have their schools.

7.) Give us adequate courts, taking things out of the hands of the police.

8.) We request cemeteries where every Protestant body can receive "a decorous, non-Catholic burial."

14.) Spaniards who request passports to go out of the country should not be denied them by Security Headquarters because they are Protestants.

15.) Give us the right to have Bibles, hymnals and liturgical books.

16.) Asks that Protestants not be denied the rights to social services unless they get parish certificates from Catholic priests.

It is true that there are a number of Protestant chapels in Spain. The figure is somewhere between 160 and 200, but one must know where they are to go to them—and to worship in private.

It is significant that there are no such fears and none of these hostile campaigns against Jews in Spain. For one thing, there are very few of them, between 4,000 and 5,000 in a population of 30,000,000. Nearly all of them live in Barcelona, some in Madrid and a few in Valencia and Seville. For another thing, neither the Catholic Church nor Government officials have any fears of Spaniards being converted to Judaism. The Jews, of course, do no proselytizing.

On the whole, barring the bigot and those who take their fascism seriously, there is no anti-Semitism in Spain. So far as I could find out there are only two synagogues in Spain, one in Barcelona and one in Madrid. They must show no outward sign of what they are. It is a safe bet that few Spaniards have ever even seen a Jew, certainly not those who live outside Madrid and Barcelona. No problem is involved for Spaniards in this respect as there is—or as they think there is—with Protestantism.

One might also believe that Freemasonry would give the Spanish authorities little anxiety. On the contrary, so far as the Caudillo, his associates and the Church hierarchy are concerned, the Freemasons are even worse than Protestants. Americans who do not know the history of European Free-masonry might be surprised at this, but Masonry in Europe was for a few centuries closely linked to free-thinking, anti-clericalism and liberalism. Many of the Republican leaders in Spain were Masons, which partly explains Franco's hatred. It will be recalled that Mussolini felt the same way, although Il Duce was not at all religious.

"Our victory," the Caudillo said in a speech at Burgos on February 27, 1939, as the Civil War was ending, "has not been over our brothers, but over the world, over international forces, over Freemasonry."

The Masons in Spain are bourgeois, middle-class and often intellectuals. There is a positive phobia against them which astonishes an American even when he knows the history of the order. As with everything, the Spaniard goes to extremes. The police are especially hard on Freemasons. They are the only people tried behind closed doors and are not even entitled to lawyers to defend them unless the Head of the Tribunal gives special permission. They can be sentenced without being brought into court.

I encountered an interesting example of the feeling toward Masons when I went to inspect the oil pipeline being laid for our air bases. All the Spaniards hired by the Americans have to be passed for security by the Spanish police. In this case the police passed any number of workers who had been Republicans, Socialists, Anarchists and Communists during the Civil War. Aside from the fact that it would have been hard to find workers who did not belong to these parties, the atmosphere in Spain has softened so much that such records no longer count. However, when the constructors asked for clearance on a certain Spanish surveyor—and they desperately needed surveyors—the police looked into his record and said, No! He was, or had been, a Freemason.

There is, it is true, a religious objection to them, too. Freemasonry had been condemned as long ago as 1738 by Pope Clement XII. In May 1950, the Bishop of Teruel in Spain published an article entitled: "The Allies and Worshippers of the Beast of the Apocalypse (Masonry, Communism and Zionism)."

He might have added Protestantism. The Bishop of Barcelona, Mgr. Gregorio Modrego, in a pastoral letter published on March 18, 1954, attributed to Protestantism the responsibility of having "opened the doors and paved the way to religious indifference, rationalism, a materialist concept of life and from there to Marxism and Communism."

To an American this seems like sheer madness but it is the sort of thing seriously and honestly believed in Spain by innumerable devout, intelligent, educated people. Yet the Roman Catholic Church is stronger today in Spain than ever before, and it always was strong. I believe one can say this in comparison, for instance, to a deeply religious time like 1492 because of our modern ways of life. Censorship today means infinitely more in this age of newspapers, radio, movies and books than it did then, and control of education means much more in an age when nearly everybody is educated.

Moreover, Ferdinand and Isabel dominated the Church. Franco certainly does not do so, as the Concordat shows. What the Caudillo does is to protect the Church, and it is a sad and bitter thing that the Catholic Church should need protection in Spain and from Spaniards.

"The Church has more to fear from political errors than from religious hatred," wrote Lord Acton (a devout Roman Catholic, incidentally) in his essay on Cavour. "In a State really free, passion is impotent against her. In a State without freedom, she is almost as much in danger from her friends as from her enemies."

It is an extraordinary institution, the Spanish Roman Catholic Church, a unique institution, great in many ways but weak in its rigidities and narrowness. It does not belong in the twentieth century and, fortunately, a whole generation of young priests is coming along, many of whom know that. There are enlightened Spanish prelates; there is the always sensible guidance of the Vatican.

Meanwhile Generalissimo Francisco Franco sits on the lid —this one, too. So long as he is there, anti-clericalism will have no chance to show its destructive power. That power, I believe, is weakening steadily. Church and people are moving toward each other for the first time. But there is a long way to go. If the Caudillo were to die tomorrow, it might go hard with the Church.

ix.

THE FUTURE

AND IF THE CAUDILLO WERE TO DIE TOMORROW, WHAT about Spain? No one is going to answer that question, and except from the point of view of a few Government officials who beat around the bush, this is the strongest indictment of all Spaniards against their Caudillo.

Spaniards do know (and a great majority are thankful for it) that there will not and cannot be another Francisco Franco. It took an extraordinary concatenation of events, including a Civil War, to produce a man who became Head of the State, Head of the Government, Commander-in-Chief of the Armed Forces and Head of the Falangist Movement, the only political organization allowed to function in Spain.

Spaniards also know, or ought to realize, that there will not and cannot be any continuation of the Franco regime. The very name, "Franco regime," is evidence of that. The regime is Franco; when he goes, it goes. There were such things as fascism, nazism, even Hitlerism and Peronism, but there is no such thing as Francoism, while Falangism withered as a doctrinal movement years ago. It has no coherent philosophy, no nationally respected leaders and it is hated and distrusted by the Army and by a majority of the workers and peasants.

The Generalissimo and his followers try to delude everybody by pointing to the "Law of Succession to the Headship of the State," passed by the customary arranged referendum on July 18, 1947. To begin with, General Franco's mandate was renewed for as long as circumstances might require—and he is the judge of the circumstances.

The traditional Monarchy was henceforth established, but "it is simply a question of awaiting the right moment to install the first King of legitimate dynasty." The Caudillo will, needless to say, choose that moment, which somehow did not materialize in the last decade. The king or a regent (Prince Juan Carlos, son of Don Juan, the Pretender, and one of the two possibilities, was only eight years old at the time) will pledge himself to uphold and continue the present basic laws of the realm—hence the supposed continuity of the regime. In any event, it is provided that the monarch should be thirty years old and Juan Carlos is barely nineteen now.

Since no one remotely expects the Generalissimo to relinquish power while he is alive and well, all this is academic. In any modern democracy it does not matter who dies; the system carries on. In a totalitarian state it does not matter greatly either, as we saw in Russia, for the dominant political party provides for continuity. In Spain there is no system and no dominant party; there is only Francisco Franco.

In June 1956, a "Commission of 37 for the study of the Fundamental Laws," composed of leaders of the Falange, Church, universities, the administration and economists was appointed. By the end of the year they had prepared two drafts for further discussion, breaking up the concentration of powers in the Dictator's hands but, naturally, whatever they recommended had to be approved by the Caudillo and, in any event, they took care to recommend that General Franco retain his present powers as long as he lives. In other words, it is a solemn farce, whatever fuss is made about it.

The Cortes, even under the new draft, would continue to be made up of members chosen, one-third from the Falange party, a third from the labor unions and the remainder made up of the mayors of the principal towns, university rectors and persons who have given outstanding service to the nation. Since the only national labor syndicate is controlled by the Falange, since the mayors are Falangists and the others are appointed by the Caudillo, one can see that this is another farce.

The Cortes are today, and would be under the new draft, an elaborate rubber stamp, of some value to discuss and criticize non-political measures but essentially powerless. Whatever laws the present Cortes prepares are accepted or not by General Franco as he pleases.

One might well ask why the Caudillo bothers, but there one gets up against the traditional Spanish mania for "legality" which has made such an indelible imprint on Latin America. The worst dictators in the New World, like Generalissimo Rafael L. Trujillo of the Dominican Republic, who can teach Franco lessons in absolutism, insist on having a Congress solemnly passing laws, regular elections, Cabinet meetings and the like.

Aside from the fact that Franco keeps and will keep absolute power as long as he can, there is the fatal impediment in Spain, that the so-called "basic laws" on which the Commission of 37 is working, do not add up to a coherent system of administration. The first thing Spain is going to do after Franco is to convoke a Constituent Assembly and draw up a valid, viable constitution.

It is quite likely that Spain will have a monarchy during or immediately after the Franco regime. Like all Spain's high military officers, General Franco is Monarchist—emotionally and theoretically. But even if he becomes one practically and chooses a king—for he will be the kingmaker if he is alive—it will mean little to the process of ruling Spain. As I pointed out before, neither Don Juan nor his son, Juan Carlos, is by any stretch of the imagination capable of ruling Spain—nor would either of them be allowed to. The chosen one would presumably be a constitutional king, without any more real power than a British Monarch. His true value and purpose would be as a symbol of unity, a steadying influence in a situation that is certainly going to be unstable and that might be chaotic. The centrifugal forces in Spain, regionalism above all, might be held in check by a monarchy.

The Caudillo has talked of a monarchy as if it could provide a continuation of his regime. He does not want the sort of "liberal and parliamentarian monarchy that was inflicted on us" in the reign of Alfonso XIII. However, he is either deluding himself or deceiving his people, since no other form of monarchy is possible in the last half of the twentieth century.

So far as Spaniards are concerned, except for some grandees, aristocrats or a few who see the monarchy in religious terms, the people could not care less whether there is a monarchy or not. The Army generals would be monarchist for the most part. The Falange is by tradition and feelings anti-monarchist but it has, perforce, accepted the Law of Succession.

The best hope for the monarchy (aside from the fact that General Franco could and would impose it whenever he wishes) lies in the fact that a king would represent a change, even if only a potential change, from the present regime. It would seem to many Spaniards like a chance for a new lease on life. There are many unhappy memories of the Second Republic among the older generation. As I said, it made a mess, and its period in office was an inefficient and chaotic one for Spain.

This does not prove that a Third Republic would not do better, or that the Second Republic failed because of its sins of mismanagement. It never really had a chance. However, those unhappy memories stick. The older men in Spain do seem discouraged. They saw the monarchy under Alfonso XIII, the dictatorship of Primo de Rivera under Alfonso, then the Second Republic, which failed and led to the Civil War, and now a dictatorship without a monarchy. Nothing worked, no system has been a success, and they see no type of government elsewhere that promises a success.

The political future looks black. On this just about all Spaniards are agreed. One Spanish friend of mine remarked ironically: "The only way we can have continuity is for Franco to live forever." If ever a man could say: "After me, the deluge!" he is Francisco Franco.

His dilemma is the classic one I mentioned before. He wants to keep power while he is alive and have his type of regime continue after his retirement or death. But in order to prepare for this continuity he would have to build up the men and the forces that would carry on. Yet, if he gives such power to any individual or group, his own power will immediately be threatened. So he remains impaled on the horns of his dilemma.

He is no different in this respect from all military rulers since history began. He not only likes his power and acts to keep it, but he persuades himself that the good of his people and nation demand that he stay in power. There is no reason to doubt his sincerity; the road to dictatorship was almost always paved with good intentions.

If no one can challenge his power, then there is no one, so far as anybody knows, capable of taking power. Therefore, there is no alternative to Franco, and even those who now oppose him might in great majority vote to keep him in power today to avoid the terrors of the unknown. Yet it is he who has created this unknown.

Of course, when General Franco dies somebody or some group must take over. It is an invariable rule with regimes of this type (Argentina is the latest outstanding example) that when the dictator goes the military must assume control. It is the only element capable of maintaining law and order. From its ranks another dictator could rise or try to rise, but no one would give such a man a chance of success in Spain today. The country deserves a better fate than another general. The days of the *caudillos* are drawing to a close.

What appalls anyone who studies the situation is this complete lack of preparation of the Spanish people to govern themselves, as they surely must do some day. For eighteen years they have had an autocrat with a horror of democracy and liberalism, a man who does not believe the people have any right to rule themselves and who has deliberately kept them, not only powerless, but in ignorance of the great movements of political freedom that began with the American and French Revolutions. The only official political philosophy that Spain has known for eighteen years is anti-communism and even communism, the enemy, is distorted for the purpose.

The result is a youth either ignorant and indifferent, or else aware of their ignorance and rebellious. General Franco has been having a good deal of trouble with university students, and he certainly deserves it. It is a great and hopeful

171

thing to see these youngsters, who have never been taught or even allowed to learn what liberalism is, turn instinctively to liberalism. Dr. Gregorio Marañon, one of the outstanding intellectuals of Spain and a true liberal, has expressed his joy and faith in the generation of university students who were born in the Civil War and brought up all their lives under the Franco regime.

When the noted Spanish philosopher, José Ortega y Gasset died in October 1955, more than 1,000 students walked to his grave in San Isidro cemetery in Madrid in tribute to this apostle of liberalism, whom the regime had muzzled. One of the students read a truly moving message of homage, almost a lament for what they are not learning and cannot learn:

"Between Ortega and ourselves there is an abyss that cannot be crossed. Every day we realize that something has been lost. Nobody tells us what to study or how. No one tells us the purpose that a university is supposed to serve, but we are sure it serves us little, and that it should be changed, root and branch."

On November 18, in the amphitheatre of the University of Madrid, Dr. Marañon pronounced a funeral oration. He told me that his talk had not been advertised in any way, and he was amazed to see 2,000 students show up. At one point he praised "the liberalism taught by the friend of my young days, Don José Ortega y Gasset." There was a tremendous ovation from the students—and yet, what could they know of liberalism?

They knew it meant freedom to learn, to think for themselves, to draw upon the great minds of other lands and other times. Free debate, free discussion of political ideas—such things have been denied to university students in the Franco regime. There has been what someone called a process of "diseducation." With minds kept so immature, in a political sense, communism is attractive rather than repellent.

Is it any wonder that we are seeing a "Rebellion of the Young" in Spain. Undoubtedly, the active rebels are a minority of the 60,000 university students, but they are a significant group. So far as sentiments are concerned, there is no doubt that a large majority are anti-Franco.

This was proved at the beginning of 1956 when the results of an official poll among students of the University of Madrid were published. It showed that 74 per cent of the students considered the Government to be incompetent and that 85 per cent accused the ruling classes of immorality. Ninety per cent thought the military hierarchy ignorant, bureaucratic and worthless; 48 per cent accused the military of being brutal, libertines and heavy drinkers. Fifty-two per cent of the students even considered the ecclesiastical hierarchy to be immoral, ostentatious and ambitious.

There were many more such results in this same poll and in the report that accompanied it. The greatest sensation, however, was provided in a sober, careful, restrained study "On the Spiritual Situation of the University Youth," written by the then Rector of Madrid University, Pedro Lain Entralgo, in December 1955. It was not for publication, but was circulated to members of the Government and Church hierarchy and other important personages. It soon got around extensively and created a furor.

It is a long document which, essentially, is devoted to analyzing "the causes of unrest" among the university students who, it is pointed out, are the first to express opinions latent in society. This is, indeed, true of Spanish as it is of most Latin students.

Lain Entralgo noted that for the students the Civil War

was simply something they heard or read about, not an experience. Those students who go abroad are attracted to the strange and new intellectual currents which they meet for the first time.

"There is not yet much sign of a movement of Marxist opinion," the Rector wrote, "but it would not be surprising if it is incubating among those whose social conscience tends towards radicalism."

Insofar as there is political unrest among the students, Lain Entralgo said, it is "mainly concerned with Spain's future and with a sharp criticism of the lack of energy of our State in trying to provide a just and effectual solution of the problems of Spanish life, especially those in the social and administrative sphere."

Among the remedies suggested was to "open the horizons" of the literary, artistic and intellectual world in and out of Spain and to do away with "indefensible" censorship.

That sort of frank and critical talk is simply not allowed in public or in print in Franco Spain. When Lain Entralgo's report was followed, in February 1956, with student riots, the Caudillo had his opportunity. Lain Entralgo went out as Rector of Madrid University and was deprived of other posts. Joaquin Ruiz Giménez, Minister of Education, was summarily dismissed. So was Raimondo Fernandez Cuesta, Secretary General of the Falange party, for the Falangists were involved in the rioting. Those responsible for the student opinion poll mentioned above were punished. Two well known cultural magazines were suppressed for a while and two key articles of the Bill of Rights were suspended for three months.

Those were the only answers that Francisco Franco had to the spiritual unrest and yearning for a broader, freer, contemporary life of the educated youth of Spain. There have been no other answers since. How could there be? Franco did not and cannot understand. Is it any wonder that we who write about Spain refer again and again to the "lid" upon which the Caudillo sits?

Early in his regime General Franco thought to control the students by the same process as he was controlling the labor unions. He gave the Falange the exclusive right to form a "University Students Syndicate" (known in Spain by its Spanish initials, SEU). Every student in theory belongs; in reality only a small minority, thinking of future jobs, pay any attention to it.

The university students are a dangerous element for Franco and they will continue to be so. A new generation always "rebels" against the old, and it should do so. That is what has made the world go round and, in so many ways, go forward. In our free countries this "Rebellion of the Young" brings fresh, provocative ideas; new blood courses through the veins of the body politic; society becomes healthier and stronger.

In a repressive dictatorship like Spain's, this normal rebellion becomes subversion, treachery, revolution; it is dangerous and even criminal. It cannot be absorbed, for it is at odds with the oppression. So it must be held down.

Yet, it is irrepressible. The university students played a great role in the overthrow of Juan Perón of Argentina. The youth of Hungary and Poland gave a marvelous account of themselves in their tragic and glorious uprisings against the Russians.

The Spanish press printed stories about Hungary, pleased and anti-communist stories. The next thing that happened was some sympathetic demonstrations of the Spanish university students. On October 6, 1956, students of the University of Barcelona in a demonstration drew the obvious conclusion and shouted for liberty, for Catalonia, and down with all dictatorships! What did Generalissimo Franco do? Just what was expected—like Philip V two centuries before, he closed the University of Barcelona.

When Dr. Marañón and others talk about the "liberalism" of the Spanish university students they are thinking of this natural, instinctive demand and urge for intellectual freedom. Without perhaps knowing it, the students are responding to a residue of true liberalism from the Second Republic which, in turn, was an intellectual derivation from the "Generation of '98." Many ideas, beliefs and hopes of the men of the Second Republic still have a strong hold on the emotions and thoughts of Spaniards. After all, the Republic lasted eight years and was a time of great intellectual ferment.

At the time of the Madrid student riots in February 1956, the Ministry of National Education publicly stated that "neither the professors nor the University are to blame for the interest shown by the nation's youth in the works of Unamuno, Ortega y Gasset, Pio Baroja, García Lorca, Hernandez, etc., but rather, responsibility lies with their parents, who possess works by these authors."

In a sense, what the Second Republic tried to do was to bring Spain into the twentieth century. This is a turbulent century, alive with intellectual, social and political ferment. Generalissimo Franco tried to shut all that out, and thanks to the Second World War, the ostracism of the foreign nations and, above all, the apathy, defeatism and pessimism of the Spanish people, worn out by their fratricidal struggle and determined to avoid another one at all costs, the Caudillo succeeded for a while—a long while in fact.

When one visits a Spanish home and in its warmth and exuberance listens to the members of the family (almost al-

ways a large family) arguing about General Franco, one gets
a sense of how the regime goes on year after year. There will
be one who argues for the Caudillo—not intellectually or
ideologically, and with the same bias for liberty with which
every Spaniard is born—but he will say something to this
effect:

"I have six [or perhaps eight] children. I have to earn my
living. I want peace. Franco keeps things going. And anyway,
I see no other solution."

He will be shouted at, but not down, by the others. No
one has a devastating answer. The young are especially critical.
They have the energy and, the elders might say, irresponsibility
to argue that freedom matters, that there is no future for the
regime or the country. One or two of the elders will look ahead
to the inevitable day of travail when General Franco dies.
None is in any sense revolutionary, and while this is a picture
of the middle class, it would be the same with the upper class
and, to a very great extent, with the working class.

Now the tide is beginning to turn. There has been something curiously static about Franco Spain which would be unusual in any country but positively abnormal for a people so
vigorous and dynamic. One has a right to ask if this is not a
moment between the extremes in which Spaniards normally
live, a suspension of animation, a pause for breath before
renewing the perpetual struggle for freedom?

Even if one argues, as many Spaniards do, that the apathy
is, itself, an evidence of Spanish extremism, a swing of the
pendulum from the exaltation of the Civil War and the years
before it, one would have to say that the pendulum is bound
to swing back sooner or later. The Caudillo acts swiftly to
smash any genuine evidence of vitality, but he is like the King
Canute of legend, ordering the tide not to come in.

The tranquility and apathy in Spain today is deceptive in a double sense. Those who say that the peacefulness is a sham or a pose or an attitude forced on the people by a heavily oppressive totalitarian police state are wrong. General Franco does not need to exert that form of oppression. However, those who think that because Spaniards are apathetic there is no deep urge to liberty and no forces capable of blowing Franco and his regime sky-high are equally wrong. As I keep saying, Spaniards are not a slow-moving, calculating people; they are emotional and explosive. They do not come in like a tide; they blow up like a volcano. The peace we see could be destroyed overnight.

The Spanish masses, because of the nature of their governments in the last 150 years (except during the Second Republic) are apart from the ruling classes. Kings, dictators, *caudillos* and governments come and go without really controlling and certainly without driving the Spanish mass. So long as that mass is quiescent, the ruler functions; when it rises the ruler is swept away. In a sense, one can say that the Spanish people are essentially more left-wing than, let us say, in England.

Just before the Minister of Education, Ruiz Jiménez, was kicked out, he made an address to the National Board of Education. It was "urgently necessary," he said, to educate the masses, and if the State did not make a great effort to do so within the next few years, they would see a result that might be "dramatic and catastrophic." Nothing has been done. The illiteracy in Spain must be the highest in Western Europe. The last official census, in 1950, listed 7,792,651 illiterates and 20,184,104 who could read and write.

The fault has lain with the middle classes. The upper classes failed Spain under the Monarchy and the middle classes under the Republic and the Franco regime. Yet the future rulers can only come from those same middle classes—the businessmen and bankers, the intellectuals, the Army officers, the hierarchy of the Church, the civil service. This class is steadily growing in size and becoming socially and economically dominant to the exclusion of the lower and upper classes.

One of the major troubles with Spaniards has been their inability to compromise. There has been no moderation, no middle ground, no tolerance, although I, for one, believe that all these things are coming and are at last evident to some degree in Spain. Meanwhile, one has to say that up to now Spain has lacked a really strong middle class, a conservatism that is not reactionary and a radicalism that is not revolutionary.

The Spaniard is fairly impervious to criticism because he is so sure that the foreigner does not and cannot understand him. Yet, the whole history of modern Spain is proof that the Spaniard does not understand himself in the sense that he cannot or has not found the answer to his own character and desires. At least, no foreigner is so critical of the Spaniard and his institutions as other Spaniards. Few countries in the modern world are so divided, so lacking in homogeneity, so difficult to hold together.

Canovas del Castillo, the nineteenth century dictator, once said: "In Spain everything frequently falls to pieces except the race." The problem has been how to give that race a political and social structure which suits its character and aspirations. Lord knows, Francisco Franco has not done so.

But has he inadvertently helped to prepare the ground? Strange as it may seem, even a critic like myself believes in the possibility of what would be an irony of history. By bringing an enforced internal peace to Spain and by keeping Spain out of World War II the Generalissimo has permitted the nation to approach a state of health that may well bring some form of democracy when he goes. It is conceivable that future historians may paradoxically find this to be the Caudillo's most positive achievement, which would be ironical because it is in no sense what he aimed at or what he wants—quite the contrary.

The Anglo-Saxon visitor to Spain, with his feeling for liberty, is naturally shocked by the Franco regime when he stops to think about it, but it is interesting how many Americans and Englishmen will rationalize their approval of the Caudillo by saying: "The Spanish people aren't ripe for democracy. They are monarchists by temperament. Our way of life wouldn't attract them. We mustn't apply our political, social and religious criteria to them."

Curiously enough, many Spaniards talk the same way, especially Franco Spaniards. As Foreign Minister Martín Artajo said: "We are original!"

Yet the argument that Spain does not have the economic and social structure to build a democracy is slowly becoming invalid. There is a maturity about the Spaniard today that is new in his history. He is more stable, more balanced, more European, more middle-class than he ever was.

Spain is at last moving in many ways into the twentieth century and becoming a European power. The days are going, or even gone when one could truly say: "Africa begins at the Pyrenees."

When the Suez Canal crisis arose at the end of July 1956, and Spain was faced with the choice of going with Europe or going with North Africa, she chose Europe, and it was the natural and even necessary choice. Foreign Minister Martín Artajo went to London in August to attend the meeting of the twenty-two user powers of the Suez Canal—the first international political conference attended by Franco Spain and hence a historic meeting for the Spaniards. It is true that Spain then and since has tried hard to keep in well with Egypt and the Arab States, for she rightly cherishes her links of friendship with the Moslem world, but the fact remains that she is and must act as a Western European power. The American military alliance would by itself make this necessary, but there are many other forces working in the same direction.

Many more Spaniards than before are going to France, Britain and Germany, and coming back with a new vision of what the outside world is like, politically and intellectually. This is a return to the civilized days of the years before the Civil War. The "Generation of '98" and the younger men who came out of it did just that. A surprising number of the Spanish Republican leaders had their higher education in Germany, above all at Heidelberg.

There is, for the first time, a great demand for news from abroad, and while the Spanish press is most selective in what it prints and how it prints the news, it does give a fair amount of space to events abroad. The literature of Western Europe and the United States is being eagerly read, above all by those who know foreign languages. Here, again, the censorship—especially the Church's censorship—severely restricts what can be translated into Spanish and published, but all things are relative and in this respect there has been a great improvement.

The whole modern trend toward "One World" is against the Generalissimo and the Church. Just as the British never forget they are an island, so the Spaniards never forget they are a peninsula, but in modern times such distinctions lose a good deal of their force. Foreigners will still be impressed with the fact that Spain is not Europe in the sense that France, Italy and Germany are, but anyone like myself who has known Spain in other years can see how fast the country is moving into the European picture as a whole.

I am sure that we Americans will give this movement much greater impetus. The Church leaders, who were so disturbed and resentful against the American military pact because it would introduce Protestants and modernity into Spain, had reason to be so from their point of view. The agreement represented a breach in the walls, just as the Napoleonic invasion did a century and a half ago and likewise the Civil War, which brought in the anti-Fascist, anti-Communist struggle from outside.

The public security that Franco brought to Spain has acted like an umbrella to shield the people from the internal storms of civic strife that played such havoc in the five years preceding the Civil War. Only a fool would deny the value of internal peace to any nation. That Spain has paid a high price for this peace in terms of the dignity of the human being and his right to be free and control his own destiny is true. But that this enforced tranquility, aided by the popular apathy, has given Spain a chance to progress along the road of economic recovery is also true. Let us note here the extent to which United States aid has played a role in this economic progress, but in Spain one is continually impressed with the way the Spaniards themselves have taken hold and are lifting the country up by its bootstraps at the same time that the United States is pulling her up from the top.

This movement has not been greatly helped by General Franco except in the negative way of letting it happen and sanctioning what his economic advisers proposed. It could not take place without his consent nor could the alliance with the

United States have taken place, so he deserves his share of the credit. Many Spaniards believe that if the economic progress continues for some years, as it promises to do, political and social problems will be infinitely easier to solve.

It has stood to reason all along that Spain could never return to health so long as her people were divided by the hatred and bitterness of the Civil War. On this score, the Caudillo deserves severe condemnation. He is an unforgiving man and to this day he has not forgiven his fellow Spaniards for defending the Second Republic and fighting against him.

There is no better sign of Franco's refusal to forgive than the costly and prominent Arch of Triumph he has just completed in Madrid at the entrance to University City where so much fighting went on during the siege of Madrid in the Civil War. To Franco it was the "War of Liberation," but is it not shameful for the victor to build a monument to his triumph over his own people? Some day the people of Spain will tear down that monument stone by stone and throw it into the Manzanares River. The monument is, in fact, greatly criticized by the people, as a useless expenditure and as a deliberate effort to rub in the fact that the Nationalist forces were victorious.

Fortunately, underneath the unforgiving rigidity of the Caudillo's attitude, a reconciliation of the Spanish people has been taking place. The Caudillo must be given credit for permitting it, and he has taken many measures to bring exiles back to Spain, to extend amnesties to those in jail, to allow ex-Republicans of all parties, even Communists to return to work in freedom. The widows of military officers on the Republican side in the Civil War, for instance, draw their Government pensions just like the widows of Nationalist officers. One cannot in fairness say that the Caudillo has done nothing to foster the reconciliation of his people, but it is true that he has done little in a positive sense and he has done much to punish his former enemies and to rub in the undoubted fact that he won and they lost. There is an element of sanctimoniousness in this attitude, for the Generalissimo is certain that he represented the forces of righteousness and the Loyalists the forces of evil.

No one can say what passions remain, for the Republicans must hide them and the Nationalists share in the general apathy. There are still many thousands in Spain who will never forgive a husband, father or brother lost, perhaps assassinated, and that bitterness will be taken to the grave. Nevertheless, each passing year brings a softening of the harshness, and the younger generation as a whole simply cannot feel or harbor the animosities of the older.

The Spaniard, anyway, has lost the extreme disdain of life that he had in the early 1930's and the Civil War. In those days he talked of killing his adversaries, and when the time came he did kill them, but in some curious but undoubted way that psychology seems to have changed. The Spanish character cannot alter, but there is no question that, politically speaking, the Spaniard is less fanatical than he was.

Spanish Republican exiles, who naturally have not lost their strong feelings, will have to take note of the change in Spain. It is one of the tragedies and the heartbreaks of exile that the country left behind changes, and the exile perforce loses touch although he cannot and often will not realize that fact. The picture of Franco Spain that is firmly believed by the exiles is distorted and in many respects false. They picture a totalitarian, police state that simply does not exist. They have no idea of the degree of tolerance that Franco permits—so long as his position and the security of his regime is not threatened. They cannot imagine the economic progress that is being made. In many respects the exiles are right, morally and politically above all, but in many respects they are quite wrong—above all in their hopes, year after year, of seeing General Franco overthrown.

Every time there is a strike; every time there is a student riot, or a drought, or the Cabinet is shuffled as on February 26, 1957, the hopes of the exiles soar far beyond any practical justification. They never realized or could believe in the solid strength of Franco's position. Their one really valid cause for hope lies, as I keep saying, in the explosive character of the Spanish people and, of course, in the death or incapacitation of the Caudillo. There need be no earth-shaking or dramatic development. We have seen again and again in Spanish history that revolutionary changes come from small and, at the time, apparently irrelevant events. The Monarchy came to an end in 1931, for instance, as a result of municipal elections. It is with good reason that Spain has been called "the land of paradox."

One thing is certain, only the small minority whose jobs and power depend on the continuity of the present system—the top Falangists, the politicians, some businessmen and bankers, some Army officers and prelates—care a hoot about the continuity of the regime. Even they, with few exceptions, must realize that the regime is not going to continue. It literally has no future, for it has no true existence and no power or impetus outside one man—Francisco Franco. As I have said, when he goes, it goes.

The great problem is the succession to the Caudillo, and at this point we all—literally all, who can think clearly and are honest with ourselves—must confess that there is no possible way of guessing the future, except the obvious fact that to begin with there must be a military leader or junta.

In the meantime, it is also true that, so long as Franco lives, one cannot be sure of anything until it happens for the simple reason that whether it happens or not depends on the will of one man—and he plays his cards close to his chest.

Everything about the future of Spain is as unpredictable as her weather, which is the most unpredictable in Europe. Spain has lived for eighteen years in a fog, seen dimly by the world and unable herself to see the world, groping slowly and peacefully toward the light. Now, at last, one sees the fog beginning to clear, and there is nothing in front of Spain but an abyss.

This is what disturbs Spaniards more than any single thing about their life and their regime. General Franco feels it, too. He has often shown that he would like to find a way out, but he is inhibited by his character, which will not permit him to let go or to change.

The only certainty for the future is in that great, wonderful and terrible tomb, the Valley of the Fallen, where Francisco Franco built for himself one of the most colossal burial places of all history. For him there is the certainty of an immolation such as Philip II alone, with his Escorial, has matched in Spanish history. For Spain there is only a question mark.

Whatever one thinks of Generalissimo Francisco Franco he is and always will be one of the towering figures of Spanish history. Yet the mark he made cannot be enduring for it has no vision. In the vital field of politics he has been the sorcerer who commanded Spanish history to remain still on April 1, 1939, when the Civil War ended. There is no dynamism in the politics of Spain. History will begin again when he dies and it will begin where he began, not where he leaves off.

X.

DA CAPO

SURELY, WE SEE NOW THAT THERE WAS NO REAL VICTOR in the Spanish Civil War. Spain lost and is still paying the price. Those of us who saw the tragedy and felt the heartache made our mistakes, but in this we had a sure instinct. It may well be that Spain, the body politic, and the brave, stoical, fiery people of Spain, could not win whatever happened. A curse had been put upon their land and they have been expiating it. Perhaps, now, the price has been paid.

I am a *revenant* in some ways, a ghost from the past, a veteran reliving through the mists of two decades the agonies and the exaltations of the battles I, too, fought, if only vicariously. In that sense I lost, like the Loyalists, for my heart and soul was with them. In another sense I claim my own victory, a moral and professional one for I still feel with all my heart that the Republican cause was just and worthy, and that the job I did as war correspondent was far and away the best of my journalistic work in a career that has now lasted thirty-five years.

Going back to Spain, as I have done three times since the Civil War, is a heartache and a joy. I had left a country of intense light and darkness, a world all black and white like Picasso's tremendous and marvelous painting of "Guernica." I returned to a gray, fuzzy Spain, strangely peaceful and apathetic. Almost one would think that the horrors and the pain, the glories and the exaltations, had been a dream, a vision of a past that had existed only because the heart was so profoundly moved and the mind clouded.

It seemed as if everything worked to darken our bright picture and blur its outlines—the role that communism has played, the hysteria that McCarthy, McCarran and their ilk had brought to American life, the decomposition of the Spanish exiles, the success of Franco in creating his anti-Communist myth, the obscurity that time invariably brings. Our terrible and wonderful Spanish Civil War is receding into a dim past for the generation that has grown up since it ended. To them it is ancient history.

And yet, in truth, it is living history. What better proof do we need than that the General who led and won the rebellion that turned into a civil war still rules Spain?

The marks of the Civil War are there to be seen, but it is getting so that one has to hunt for them. In Barcelona one notes the scars pocking the buildings down at the port. The head waiter at a well-known restaurant that foreign correspondents once frequented recalls those days discreetly, and vividly remembers the first great blitz of a modern city, on St. Patrick's Day in 1938, and the day after, when Italian bombers came from Italy, Sardinia and the Balearics.

The Plaza Catalunya subway station has been changed now beyond all recognition, with shops and lunch counters. When I last saw it, as Barcelona was falling, the whole great station, tracks and all, was jammed with thousands of women, children and old folks taking refuge against the merciless and incessant bombing raids of the last four days before the city fell.

The Diagonal, where the International Brigades made their last parade and where the Navarrese Brigades marched in at the end is now officially named the Avenida de General-issimo Franco—but everybody still calls it the Diagonal. Barcelona has more than doubled in population; its total is now nearly 2,000,000. There are new buildings everywhere, and somehow it seems natural that the war has no physiognomy there today. Barcelona, on the whole, never really cared.

Madrid did, and that is why it comes as a shock to find Madrid so apathetic. The building boom has made the capital hardly recognizable. One goes in search of the old landmarks of the siege of Madrid, days when the capital seemed the hub of the universe. The Telefonica building hardly shows its scars, but those who look for them can see where the damage from hundreds of shells has been repaired.

On the Gran Via the Cafe Molinero has gone from its corner. El Chicote (which figures in Hemingway's "The Fifth Column)" is still there, but hideously remodelled and modernized. The Florida Hotel is hardly recognizable, but those of us who lived there during the shelling will know that the new marble on the street floor, the bright marble pillars on the façade above and the shutters are all replacements where the shelling had made gaping holes or scars. In the Civil War, Ernest Hemingway stayed in a room on the third floor under jutting balconies, as I did. He wrote "The Fifth Column" there. It was his theory that we had a "dead angle" from the German artillery firing over the hotel at the Telefonica. When the shells fell short, the Florida was hit. The concierge's desk has been moved, but it is the same concierge—a man most unwilling to talk and not to be blamed for his reticence.

The façade of the National Palace is still badly scarred. From its courtyard one looks across toward Garabitas Hill, where the German artillery covered the narrow channel of communications between the Nationalist lines on the far side of the Manzanares River and University City, a bridgehead held at great cost by the Rebels all through the war. It was their one foothold inside Madrid and they held it, perhaps for prestige, perhaps out of Spanish pride.

Down below in the Casa de Campo and the Prado the trenches have all been filled in. Looking up from it now one sees the new red-and-white buildings of University City in place of the broken, bombed and shelled wrecks that Franco's forces held. This was the front line, the most famous of the war, and a symbol of the stubborn courage that animated both sides. During one April week in 1937, Hemingway and a few others among us climbed day after day into a bomb-wrecked apartment house on the Paseo de Rosales to watch a Loyalist drive against Garabitas Hill and the Rebel bottleneck. It was a vain attempt to pinch off the University City salient.

Now it is hard to believe that these neat paths and roads, the young trees and green grass, the flowers, the children playing while their mothers and nurses watch, that once this was a scene of constant and sudden death, and a certain degree of glory for Spaniards and—at one highly critical moment—for the foreigners of the International Brigades.

The Montaña Barracks, once the main garrison building of Madrid, is gone. General Franco pulled it down, doubtless for the same reason that Louis XVI might have pulled down the Bastille if the Revolution had been suppressed. It was the storming of the Montaña Barracks by the poorly armed civilians and private soldiers of Madrid that saved the capital for the Republic in the first days of the rebellion.

The tourists who are pouring into the Prado Museum in Madrid would never know the danger those famous paintings ran into during the Civil War and the vast amount of trouble and expense the Republican Government took to save them.

Adolfo Rupérez, then head of the Calcografía Nacional, as an introduction to his extraordinary Civil War edition of the etchings of Goya (almost certainly the last that will ever be made from the original plates), composed an engraving of his own showing where high explosive and incendiary bombs and artillery shells fell on and around the Academy of Fine Arts where these and many other priceless plates, engravings and books were kept. The treasures were all saved and Rupérez, himself, turned over the Goya plates to the Nationalists when Madrid fell. They are safe in the Calcografía Nacional today, but it is one of the mysteries of the art world as to what happened to the greater part of the etchings that Señor Rupérez told me he did. He thought they went to London for sale, but I checked carefully on that and found it was not the case.

So far as the Prado treasures were concerned, they are all back and without even a scratch of damage. The Republicans sent the pictures and movable statues, carefully crated, to Switzerland in days when their armies were in great distress. It has been one of the truly petty meannesses of the Franco regime that far from giving credit to these Spaniards who saved their artistic patrimony at great cost, the Nationalists acted as if the Loyalists were trying to steal and sell the treasures. A lack of magnanimity has been an extraordinary feature of the Franco regime.

It is in the battlefields around Madrid that veterans like myself can best relive the stirring days of the siege of Madrid and the Insurgent efforts to capture it and end the war.

The American Battalion of the International Brigade got its baptism of fire in February 1937, down on the Jarama River, southeast of Madrid. The Rebels were trying to cut the Valencia highway about fifteen miles from Madrid at a point where there was a bridge across the Arganda River. The Nationalists came close enough to get the highway under machine-gun fire and make life risky for war correspondents, but they never did cut that highway.

The Jarama River flows south to join the Tagus. There is a flat strip between hills running eastward with Morata in the back where International Brigade headquarters were. The land is now full of fine olive trees and the keen Castilian wind blows across fields of wheat. The hills toward the river were the natural line of defense where the Republicans had to hold and where later they tried a number of minor offensives—as did the Rebels.

It was in those bleak, eroded hills that the Americans first went into action. Their trenches and dugouts are still there, partly filled by the drift of the years, but all clearly outlined. For those who were there when it was swarming with troops and crackling with danger there are ghosts on the bare, silent, windswept hills now, ghosts of all nationalities, but to me, above all, ghosts of the Americans whose memory still gives me a thrill of pride.

The most famous of the Republican victories came in the following month of March—the Battle of Guadalajara. It was there that Mussolini's Italians made their ill-fated thrust and received one of the most ignominious defeats in the history of united Italy. Fortunately for them, a handful of brave Internationals of the Garabaldini Battalion fought with the Spanish Loyalists and showed the true mettle of Italians when they fight for something they know and believe in.

The Fascist Italians came down the Barcelona-Madrid highway from Saragossa, aiming for Guadalajara, after which they would have had plain sailing down the flat valley of the Henares River to Madrid. Four divisions of what the Italians officially called "Voluntary Legions" confidently drove down. It was an expeditionary force, fully equipped as Blackshirt militia. Those of us who talked to prisoners after the battle learned that many of them thought they were going to Africa when they sailed. In a war that until then had been fought by small columns, poorly equipped and armed on both sides, but especially on the Loyalist side, this army of Italians was far superior to anything that had yet been seen. Rarely in the history of modern times has pride taken such a fall!

Guadalajara has changed little (actually the Italians never got within twenty miles of it, although the town gave its name to the battle). The chief memento of that time—and it is an eternally sad one—is the completely gutted Renaissance palace of the Duke of Infantado. I watched it burn during one of the first nights of the battle, but I wanted to hear what the old official guide was telling visitors nowadays and I asked him what had happened. "Airplanes," he said, "with incendiary bombs." He was right. Guadalajara had been bombed that day and everyone took it for granted the planes were Italian. The famous Patio of the Lions still stands, but it is wide open to the skies. Here and there some of the ceilings and frescoes are partly existing to show how beautiful the palace once was. The ornate, stone-studded façade of the typically Renaissance walls of the palace stand today as always, but the inside, having been of wood, burned like a torch.

193

One drives on, past the villages of Taracena and Torrija, where Lister and Modesto, commanders of the *Quinta Armata* —the Fifth Army—a purely Spanish force that had just been fully organized and trained, had their headquarters during the six days of the battle. Beyond Torrija there is a side road that leads down to Brihuega, where the real battle was fought and the Italians broke and ran. Here the flat terrain is first cut into rough hills that crowd the road and then to deeply indented, stony land. One remembers those stones vividly because every time a shell struck the ground it drove stones out like so many deadly pieces of shrapnel. This was the place to stop the Italians or lose Madrid and with it the Civil War.

Then one comes on the *cuenca,* or hollow, with the ancient little grey village of Brihuega down on the far side. The Italians had come into Brihuega, plastered their stencilled Fascist signs over the walls, along with *"Vivas"* for Il Duce, and were using the place temporarily as a headquarters for one of their divisions. Their line, which thrust forward like so many tentacles along this road, the main highway and the road to Cifuentes north of it, had come smoothly forward until Lister met them with a shock at about Kilometer 83 or 84 of the Madrid highway and jarred that column back on its heels. In the fighting of the next few days the two divisions in the van were somewhat mauled and demoralized and were replaced by the two remaining divisions. It was then that the Republicans, who were getting advice from some Russians or at least Russian-trained staff officers and who had brought up a small contingent of International Brigaders, made a counter-attack at Brihuega.

The result was a complete rout. Those of us who came up in the morning could hardly believe our eyes. The ground was strewn for miles around with Italian rifles and machine-guns,

Italian ammunition, stores of all kinds, Italian motorcycles, trucks and cars, dead bodies (surprisingly few) and I saw many Italian prisoners who talked freely and aggrievedly of what had happened to them. That was the first time the world had learned the extent of Italian intervention in a war in which Britain and France had imposed the legal fiction—and maintained it on their side—of "non-intervention." The story seemed so extraordinary that my account of it was not believed by the Night Managing Editor who thereby perpetrated an editorial boner that became famous in the history of *The New York Times.*

The defeat was a tremendous shock to the Duce's pride. He was at that time in Libya on a white horse preparing to receive the "Sword of Islam." He dismounted quickly, so to speak, and hopped a plane back to Rome, where he set about trying to repair the damage. One way he did it was by regrouping the forces and getting General Franco to let him send them later against the then exhausted and almost defenseless Asturian zone in the North.

Another way was to re-write history in the fashion made so commonplace since then by Fascist and Communist propagandists. Guadalajara was calmly rated as an Italian victory and it figures as such in Ciano's Memoirs. I doubt that many Italians to this day know the truth. At the time it was certainly kept from the people of Italy while all Spain—literally all Spain, Nationalist as well as Loyalist, and all Europe—laughed.

One still finds some tangible evidence of this historic fiction. There are two monuments to the Italians along the main highway, one well back of where the fighting took place and the other at Kilometer 83.5, which was almost exactly where the Italian drive was stopped. The inscription tells how Console General Alberto Liuzzi (the Blackshirt military equivalent of a general) gave his life "rather than yield to the enemies of Roman civilization." It appears that he fell "among you people in the irresistible impetus of his Fascist faith." Like the monument to Shelley's Ozymandius, it stands solitary and eroded beside the lonely highway, weathered by the fierce Castilian wind that has all but erased the word "*fede*" (faith). It is well that this monument should remain there forever as a broken symbol of the false pride of Italian Fascism.

When I said to the driver of my hired car—a Madrileño —"The Italians were stopped just about here," he gleefully replied, "Not stopped! They ran!"

So they did, and if one remembers the battle today it is in part because it was a historic and symbolic defeat, which I and others had called the "Bailén of Fascism," for it was at Bailén, as I have stated, that Napoleon's troops received their first defeat in Europe, and it was at Guadalajara that fascism received its first defeat.

It is strange to visit Brihuega nowadays—an utterly peaceful Brihuega. The Italian symbols and slogans are gone. Franco's image and the yoke-and-arrows symbol of the Falange have taken their places. One might almost forget the Civil War except for the fact that the evidences of bomb damage are still there. I was in Brihuega with Ernest Hemingway during two terrible raids. The village was an inferno that day. So there is no need to ask the men who stand in groups or the women going in and out of church, what they think. Whatever happens, they will never, for themselves or their children's children, want to play another such role in history.

The Italians would surely feel the same way if they had stood, as a group of us did one of those days, on the flat space of threshing ground between the highway and the village of Trijueque, which was within shelling range of the Italians after their retreat. We were watching the bodies of Italians being tossed into empty trucks like so many sacks of grain. A flock of sheep was browsing there when I revisited it, guarded by a Castilian shepherd, bundled in rough clothes, grave, courteous, dignified, the symbol of peace. There will always be just such sheep and just such shepherds in the inhospitable lands around Guadalajara. Foreign armies have come up and down that way since the Carthaginians and Romans. There were the Flemings of Emperor Charles V, the French of Napoleon, the Italians of Mussolini—but the end result was and always will be a Castilian shepherd guarding his flock.

For Spaniards fed and brought up on the version of the Civil War taught by the Franco regime, the greatest sanctuary and the greatest symbol of the Civil War always will be the Alcázar of Toledo. It was there that some 1,500 Spaniards of the garrison and Civil Guard with the women of the town and their children withstood a desperate siege of seventy-two days until relieved, on September 18, 1936, by General Franco himself. The ruin dominates the town today as the building itself once did. But a great new Alcázar is being completed directly across the Tagus River.

Like most people—perhaps nearly everybody in and out of Spain—I was content to accept the Franco version of the siege of Alcázar, despite gnawing doubts. It did seem a bit too good to be true, and it also simply did not fit the psychology of the Loyalists as I knew them—but I accepted it. I have since got the other side of the story from two of the leading figures among the Republicans who took part in the siege—

Luis Quintanilla, the artist, and General José Asensio, both American citizens now. I also made some inquiries on my last trip to Spain.

First for the Franco version, which is so famous. It is presented in its most vivid form when one goes around nowadays on the guided tour of the old Alcázar in Toledo. One comes to the office of the then Col. Juan Moscardó, nominal commander of the garrison. On July 23, 1936, in the first week of the siege, a Loyalist militia commander telephoned him from Madrid, the guide tells us. He gave the Colonel ten minutes to agree to surrender. "If not," he said, "I am going to shoot your son Luis whom I hold here in my power."

Luis, 16 years old, came to the phone, and said merely, "Papa."

"What's happening, my son?" Colonel Moscardó asked.

"*Nada*—nothing—they say they are going to shoot me if you don't surrender the Alcázar."

"Well then, commend your soul to God, cry '*Viva España!*' and die like a patriot."

The telephones they are supposed to have used stand beneath their portraits. It all seemed in the best—and worst—Spanish tradition. The tombs of the 104 men of the garrison who died and were buried in a sanctuary inside the Alcázar contains an inscription that reads: "A people who can count on men like those who lie here is invincible."

Let us grant the sentiment, which is true enough, but what about the story?

In the first place, Moscardó's son, then an ordinary soldier of nineteen, not sixteen, was one of those who had taken refuge in the Montaña Barracks in Madrid in the first days of the war. The barracks were stormed and most of the soldiers and officers inside—except those who turned against their officers and joined the Republicans, and Luis Moscardó was not one of these—were killed in the fighting or shot afterward. This was on July 19, 1936, four days before the Alcázar incident is supposed to have taken place. No one took the trouble to identify Luis's body, for obvious reasons. His father was not then in any way known and, in fact, Colonel Moscardó never was the real military commander in the Alcázar. The commander was a Colonel José Abeilhe, the director of the Infantry Academy in the Alcázar. Colonel Moscardó was merely Director of the *Escuela Central de Gimnasia* in Toledo, but he outranked Abeilhe and hence had nominal command during the siege. The overwhelming chances are that Luis Moscardó was already dead when his father took refuge in the Alcázar and there is every reason to believe that Colonel Moscardó only learned of his son's death after the relief of the Alcázar.

The family of Colonel Abeilhe, incidentally, was in Madrid all during the siege and was not molested in any way, although Abeilhe was the real traitor of the incident. He had assured headquarters in Madrid that he was loyal and would hold the Alcázar for the Government. Instead, as learned later, he was in the Rebel plot and was preparing all along to fight against the Republicans.

Another fact which contradicts the famous story is that the telephones, along with the water, gas and electricity, connecting the Alcázar with the rest of the city of Toledo were cut on July 22nd, and remained cut from then on. Communication was thereafter maintained by means of loud speakers. How, therefore, could Luis Moscardó have telephoned his father from Madrid on July 23rd?

The absurdity of using this one hostage to achieve the surrender of the Alcázar ought also to be noted. Even if the story were true and even if he had wanted to yield, Colonel Moscardó would have been powerless to do so with all the other officers present who knew that their lives would be forfeit if they were captured. The Moscardó story presupposes a naiveté and stupidity on the part of the Loyalists which are simply incredible.

I am boiling a complicated and historic event down to its bare bones, but there is one other feature that must be noted.

The women and children who were in the Alcázar all during the siege—some 570 of them—were without question lured and stampeded into the fortress either in ignorance or against their will. Moreover, the Loyalists made repeated attempts, with the most iron-clad guarantees of safety, to get the Rebels to let the women and children out. These poor creatures were quite simply hostages of the Rebels, held against their will. Far from being a source of pride to the Nationalists, their presence and their sufferings represent one of the most shameful incidents of the Civil War on the Franco side.

When the Alcázar was relieved on September 18, 1936, the Rebel command imposed a strict, two-day censorship on the press and photographers which explains why there are so few extant photographs of the evacuation of the fortress. Presumably, the Nationalists were ashamed of the spectacle of the women and children they had held. However, the news of their sufferings got around and, fortunately for posterity, Spain's famous and outspoken philosopher, Miguel de Unamuno, got the story in Salamanca at first hand from two nuns who had been in the Alcázar all through the siege, acting as nurses, and who were outraged by what had happened. Unamuno was the first, but by no means the last, to protest.

Between September, when the Alcázar was relieved, and November, not a word was said about the incident of Moscardó, his son and the telephone. Is this not strange?

Perhaps the inspiration for this famous story came from a tale in Spanish history, taught to all children and a source of pride to centuries of Spaniards. This occurred in 1294 at Tarifa, near Cadiz, where the great soldier Alonso Pérez de Gúzman, surnamed "the Good," was defending the port against the Moors. The enemy presented themselves before the walls with Gúzman's son as their prisoner, held in plain sight. They said that either the town must be yielded instantly, or they would kill his son. Gúzman contemptuously drew his own dagger and flung it at them, telling them to kill his son with that.

It is, perhaps, a shame to destroy a wonderful story like that of the Alcázar, but I firmly believe history is going to do so as surely as it did the myth of George Washington and the cherry tree. I have gone to this length to do so here because so far as I know, the true story has never before been told, certainly not in English.

There are lots of true stories about the Spanish Civil War that remain to be told by the historians of future generations. Only they will be able to sift the wheat from the chaff, the true from the false, to weigh the good and the bad, to lay the blame or mete out the praise. We are too close to it. Many facts are not yet available, and those we have are clouded by our emotions.

I would never dream of hiding my own bias or denying it. I did not do so during the Spanish Civil War and I do not do so now. In my credo, as I said before, the journalist is not one who must be free of bias or opinions or feelings. Such a newspaperman would be a pitiful specimen, to be despised

rather than admired. There is only one test that means anything, only one quality that the reader has a right to demand—
the truth as the man sees it and all the truth. He must never
change or suppress that truth; he must never present as the
truth anything that he does not honestly believe to be true.

We journalists are lucky, sometimes. We live history and
we often provide the material for future historians. To me—
professionally speaking—the Spanish Civil War was my greatest moment. My interpretation of it may, of course, be wrong.
It is not the popular interpretation of after years, in or out
of Spain.

One of my first journalistic experiences after the Civil
War had ended in 1939, was to stand in an official box in
Naples (I had been transferred to Rome by *The Times*) and
watch a long parade of Italian "volunteers" from Spain pass
in review before Count Ciano and the Spanish Foreign
Minister, Ramón Serrano Suñer. This was a victory parade by
tens of thousands of fully equipped Italian soldiers who had
fought for Franco while the British and French observed their
so-called "non-intervention" and the United States kept its
disgraceful arms embargo. Then I went to my typewriter
and duly sent a description of the event to *The New York
Times*.

Such is journalism, such is life, such is history. Only time
straightens it all out, and when that day comes I know the
verdict and the laurels will not go to Francisco Franco Bahamonde and the generals who rose with him against their
legal Government. It will go to those who strove, however
feebly and inefficiently and who fought so bravely for principles and ideals which were the same as most of us cherish—
the freedoms of the individual, the rights and dignity of man,
a liberal, democratic state. They lost, but it would be a rash

commentator and prophet who said that Franco and his ilk really won.

No doubt they won a good deal for themselves, personally. But eighteen years are not long in the history of a nation, least of all a nation that was great centuries before Christ walked in Jerusalem. A race formed from Iberians, Celts, Carthaginians, Romans, Jews, Moors, the mysterious Basques, the European Catalans—such a race has roots too deep to be shaken by a little man on a white horse.

Often in going around one senses that grave weight of the centuries, the eternal Spain. I remember standing in Segovia not so long ago below its breath-taking Alcázar that seemed poised to soar like some huge ship into the air. Here was a town virtually untouched by the Civil War, untouched, it seemed, by all that had gone before—the ancient days, the era of Spanish greatness, the decline in modern times. There are many families in Segovia today whose *hidalgo* ancestors went with the Spanish conquerors to the New World. Civil Wars pass it by; *caudillos* come and go, but the true, immemorial Spain goes on.

Lots of things have changed in Spain during the past eighteen or twenty years, but not the breed. The Spaniard is a man of principle, a believer to the death in virtues like honor, courage, good name and, above all, in his right to be a free man.

One change there is from those Civil War days that does, indeed, warm the heart. We used to say, *"Salud!"* on meeting and parting. Now everybody says, *"Adios!"*—God be with you.